# KEY FACTS

# CRIMINAL LAW

## THIRD EDITION

## JACQUELINE MARTIN

## Hodder Arnold

A MEMBER OF THE HODDER HEADLINE GROUP

Orders: please contact Bookpoint Ltd, 130 Milton Park, Abingdon, Oxon OX14 4SB.
Telephone: (44) 01235 827720. Fax: (44) 01235 400454. Lines are open from 9.00–5.00,
Monday to Saturday, with a 24-hour message answering service. You can also order through
our website www.hoddereducation.co.uk

*British Library Cataloguing in Publication Data*
A catalogue record for this title is available from The British Library.

ISBN: 978 0340 94030 3

First published 2001
Second Edition published 2004
Third Edition published 2007
Impression number     10   9   8   7   6   5   4   3   2
Year                  2011  2010  2009  2008  2007

Copyright © 2001, 2004, 2007 Jacqueline Martin

Hachette's policy is to use papers that are natural, renewable and recyclable products and made
fromwood grown in sustainable forests. The logging and manufacturing processes are expected
to conform to the environmental regulations of the country of origin.

Typeset by Transet Limited, Coventry.
Printed in Great Britain for Hodder Arnold, an imprint of Hodder Education, an Hachette
Livre UK Company, 338 Euston Road, London NW1 3BH by Cox & Wyman Ltd.,
Reading, Berkshire.

# CONTENTS

# PREFACE

The Key Facts series is designed to give a clear view of each subject. This will be useful to students when tackling new topics and is invaluable as a revision aid. Most chapters open with an outline in diagram form of the points covered in that chapter. The points are then developed in list form to make learning easier. Supporting cases are given throughout by name and for some complex areas the facts of cases are given to reinforce the point being made.

Some areas of criminal law are very complex and this book helps students by breaking down each topic into key points. This is done for both the important general principles such as *actus reus* and *mens rea* as well as for specific offences. The topics covered make it a useful resource for criminal law components of degree courses, ILEX courses and A level specifications.

This third edition has been updated with all key developments in the law. In particular, Chapter 1 brings together a number of cases involving human rights. It also contains the Privy Council case of *A-G for Jersey v Holley* (2005) on provocation. Finally, it should be noted that the Fraud Bill referred to in Chapter 13 has now become law as the Fraud Act 2006.

The law is stated as I believe it to be at 1st November 2006.

# CHAPTER 1
## INTRODUCTION TO CRIMINAL LAW

## 1.1 PURPOSE OF CRIMINAL LAW

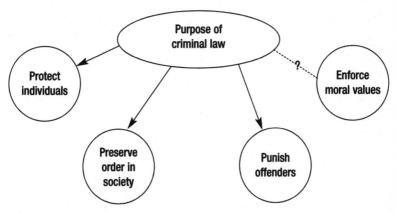

The main purposes are:

1. Protect individuals and their property from harm.
2. Preserve order in society.
3. Punish those who deserve punishment. But note that there are also other aims when sentencing offenders. These include incapacitation, deterrence, reformation and reparation.

### 1.1.1 Should the law enforce moral values?

This area is controversial. It is argued that it is not the function of criminal law to interfere in the private lives of citizens unless it is necessary to try to impose certain standards of behaviour. The Wolfenden Committee (1957) felt that intervention in private lives should only be:

- to preserve public order and decency;
- to protect the citizen from what is offensive or injurious; and
- to provide sufficient safeguards against exploitation and corruption of others, particularly those who are especially vulnerable.

Lord Devlin in the *Enforcement of Morals* (1965) disagreed. He felt that 'there are acts so gross and outrageous that they must be prevented at any cost'.

## 1.1.2 Conflicting cases

The courts are not always consistent in their approach to this area of law.

*Brown* (1993): The House of Lords upheld convictions for assault causing actual bodily harm (s47 Offences against the Person Act 1861) and malicious wounding (s20 Offences against the Person Act 1861) for acts done in private by a group of consenting adult sado-masochists.

*Wilson* (1996): The Court of Appeal quashed a conviction for assault causing actual bodily harm (s47 Offences against the Person Act 1861) where a husband had branded his initials on his wife's buttocks, at her request.

# 1.2 DEFINING A CRIME

1. A crime is conduct forbidden by the State and to which a punishment has been attached because the conduct is regarded by the State as being criminal.
2. The statement above is the only definition which covers all crimes.
3. What conduct is criminal will, therefore, vary from country to country, and from one time to another. The law is likely to change when there is a change in the values of Government and society.

## 1.2.1 Example of the changing nature of criminal law

- The Criminal Law Amendment Act 1885 criminalised consensual homosexual acts between adults in private.
- The Sexual Offences Act 1967 decriminalised such behaviour between those aged 21 and over.

- The Criminal Justice and Public Order Act 1994 decriminalised such behaviour for those aged 18 and over.
- In 2000 the Government reduced the age of consent for homosexual acts to 16, though the Parliament Acts had to be used as the House of Lords voted against the change in the law.

## 1.2.2 Judicial law-making

1. Some conduct is criminalised not by the State but by judges.
2. An example is the offence of outraging public decency which has never been enacted by Parliament. It is an invention of the judges, yet people can be convicted of it. (*Gibson* (1991))
3. Marital rape has also been criminalised by the decisions of judges. (*R v R* (1991))
4. See also the cases of *Brown* (1993) and *Wilson* (1996) in 1.1.2.

# 1.3 CLASSIFICATION OF OFFENCES

There are many ways of classifying offences depending on the purpose of the classification.

## 1.3.1 Classification by where a case will be tried

One of the most important ways of classifying offences is by the categories that affect where and how a case will be tried. For this purpose offences are classified as:

1. Indictable only offences which must be tried on indictment at the Crown Court (e.g. murder, manslaughter, rape).
2. Triable either way offences which can be tried either on indictment at the Crown Court or summarily at the Magistrates' Court (e.g. theft, burglary, assault occasioning actual bodily harm).
3. Summary offences which can only be tried at the Magistrates' Court (e.g. assaulting a policeman in the execution of his duty, common assault).

## 1.3.2 Categories for police powers of detention

1. Police powers to detain a suspect who has been arrested depend on the category of offence. There are three categories:
   - summary offences;
   - indictable offences;
   - terrorism offences.
2. For summary offences the police can only detain an arrested person for a maximum of 24 hours.
3. For indictable offences the suspect can be detained for 24 hours but this can be extended to 36 hours by an officer of the rank of superintendent or above. The police then have the right to apply to a magistrate for permission to detain the suspect for up to a maximum of 96 hours.
4. A person arrested on suspicion of terrorism offences can be detained for 48 hours. After this an application can be made to a judge to extend the detention up to a maximum of 28 days (Terrorism Act 2000, Schedule 8 as amended by the Terrorism Act 2006).

## 1.3.3 Classifying law by its source

Law comes from different sources. This is important from an academic point of view. These sources are:

- common law (judge-made);
- statutory (defined in an Act of Parliament);
- regulatory (set out in delegated legislation).

## 1.3.4 Classifying by the type of harm caused by the crime

When studying criminal law it is usual to study offences according to the type of harm caused. The main categories here are:

- offences against the person;
- offences against property;
- offences against public order.

# 1.4 ELEMENTS OF A CRIME

| ACTUS REUS<br>physical element | + | MENS REA<br>fault element | = | OFFENCE |
|---|---|---|---|---|

1. For all crimes, except crimes of strict liability (see Chapter 4), there are two elements which must be proved by the prosecution. These are:

   - *actus reus*;
   - *mens rea.*

2. These terms come from a Latin maxim *actus non facit reum nisi mens sit rea* which means the act itself does not constitute guilt unless done with a guilty mind.

3. *Actus reus* has a wider meaning than an act as it can cover omissions or a state of affairs.

4. The term *actus reus* has been criticised as misleading. Lord Diplock in *Miller* (1983) preferred the term 'prohibited conduct'. The Law Commission in the Draft Criminal Code (1989) used the term 'external element'.

5. *Mens rea* translates as 'guilty mind' but this is also misleading. The levels of 'guilty mind' vary (see Chapter 3). The Law Commission in the Draft Criminal Code (1989) used the term 'fault element'.

6. The *actus reus* and *mens rea* will be different for different crimes.

7. The *actus reus* and the *mens rea* must be present together, but if there is an on-going act, then the existence of the necessary *mens rea* at any point during that act is sufficient (*Fagan v Metropolitan Police Commissioner* (1969)). This also applies where there is a sequence of events or acts (*Thabo Meli* (1954), *Le Brun* (1991)).

8. For crimes of strict liability the prosecution need only prove the *actus reus*; no mental element is needed for guilt. (See Chapter 4 for strict liability.)

9. Even where the *actus reus* and *mens rea* are present the defendant may be not guilty if he has a defence. (See Chapter 8 for general defences.)

# 1.5 BURDEN AND STANDARD OF PROOF

1. The burden is on the prosecution to prove the case. This means that they must prove both the required *actus reus* and the required *mens rea* (*Woolmington v DPP* (1935)). An accused person is presumed innocent until proven guilty.
2. The standard of proof is 'beyond reasonable doubt'.
3. If the defendant raises a defence then it is for the prosecution to negate that defence. In *Woolmington* the defendant stated that the gun had gone off accidentally, thus raising the defence of accident. The prosecution were obliged to disprove this if the defendant was to be found guilty.
4. For certain defences the burden of proof is on the defendant. For example, for the defence of insanity the defendant has to prove he was insane at the time of the offence. Placing the burden of proof on the defence may breach Art 6(2) of the European Convention on Human Rights (see 1.6.2).
5. Where the defendant has to prove a defence the standard is the civil one of balance of probabilities.

# 1.6 CRIMINAL LAW AND HUMAN RIGHTS

1. The Human Rights Act 1998 incorporated the European Convention on Human Rights into our law. All Articles have to be considered in English law.
2. In criminal law the most relevant rights under the convention are:
   ● the right to a fair trial (Art 6(1));
   ● the presumption of innocence (Art 6(2));
   ● no punishment without law (Art 7(1)).

**3.** Other Convention rights relevant to criminal law include:
- the right not to be subjected to inhuman or degrading treatment (Art 3(1));
- the right of respect for a person's private life (Art 8);
- that, in the application of the Convention rights and freedoms, there should be no discrimination on the grounds of sex, race, colour, religion or political opinion (Art 14).

## 1.6.1 The right to a fair trial

**1.** This right is contained in Article 6(1).
**2.** In *G* (2006) it was held that the fact that the offence was one of strict liability did not render the trial unfair.

## 1.6.2 Burden of proof

**1.** Article 6(2) states that 'Everyone charged with a criminal offence shall be presumed innocent until proven guilty'. This places the burden of proof on the prosecution.
**2.** Defences which place the burden of proving the defence in the defendant may be in breach of this Article.
**3.** However, the courts have held that in some statutes the reverse burden of proof may be interpreted as evidential only (*A-G Reference (No 4 of 2002)* (2004)).
**4.** In addition, the House of Lords has held that a full reverse burden of proof may be acceptable if it is not unfair or disproportionate (*Sheldrake v DPP* (2005)).

## 1.6.3 No punishment without law

**1.** Article 7(1) states that 'No one shall be held guilty of any criminal offence on account of any act or omission which did not constitute a criminal offence under national law or international law at the time it was committed'.
**2.** If the offence is one which conforms to the fundamental objectives of the Convention, then it will not be in breach of

this Article: *CR v UK* (1996) where the conviction of a husband for the rape of his wife was approved by the European Court of Human Rights.

3. In other cases there have been challenges under Art 7 on the basis that the offence is too uncertain or lacks clarity, e.g gross negligence manslaughter (*R v Misra; R v Srivastava* (2004)) (see 9.4.2) and public nuisance (*Goldstein* (2005)). To date no challenge on the basis of lack of clarity has been successful.

## 1.6.4 Other human rights

1. There have been challenges to the criminal law on the basis of other rights in the Convention.

2. In *Altham* (2006) the defendant claimed that the refusal to allow him the defence of necessity in respect of his use of cannabis for extreme physical pain was a breach of Art 3 which provides that no one shall be subjected to 'inhuman or degrading treatment'. This challenge failed.

3. Similarly, in *Quayle* (2005) the defendant argued that the refusal to allow him the defence of necessity in respect of his use of cannabis for extreme physical pain was a breach of Art 8. This Article gives a right to respect for a person's private life. This challenge also failed.

4. In *G* (2006) the Court of Appeal accepted that there could, in some circumstances, be an infringement of Art 8(1) if a boy under 16 was prosecuted under s5 Sexual Offences Act 2003 when he had had consensual sex with a girl under 13.

5. In *Dehal* (2005) it was held that D's right to freedom of expression (Art 10) had been infringed when he was prosecuted under s4 of the Public Order Act 1986 for placing a notice in a temple stating that the preacher was a hypocrite.

## 1.6.5 Human rights and criminal procedure

1. The procedure in a case where the defendant is thought to be unfit to plead was amended after it was held in *H* (2003) that

s4A of the Criminal Procedure (Insanity) Act 1964 was not compatible with the European Convention on Human Rights.

2. Procedure for trying child defendants was altered after the European Court of Human Rights held there was a breach of Art 6 on the right to a fair trial in *T v UK: V v UK* (2000).

# CHAPTER 2

# ACTUS REUS

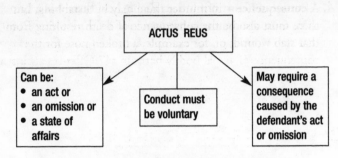

## 2.1 THE PHYSICAL ELEMENT

1. The *actus reus* is the physical element of a crime. It can be:
   - an act;
   - a failure to act (an omission);
   - a state of affairs (very rare).
2. For some crimes the act or omission must also result in a consequence.

### 2.1.1 Examples

1. **An act** – picking up an item in a shop (one way of committing the physical element for theft); or punching a victim which could be part of the physical element of an assault occasioning actual bodily harm (s47 Offences against the Person Act 1861).
2. **An omission** – failing to provide a specimen of breath; or wilful neglect of a child (i.e. failing to provide one's child with food, clothing or medical care under s1 Children and Young Persons Act 1933).
3. **A state of affairs** – being found drunk in a public place. Merely being drunk and in a public place is sufficient (*Winzar v Chief Constable of Kent* (1983)). Also *Larsenneur* (1933)

in which an alien was brought back to the United Kingdom by Irish police. On her arrival she was arrested and charged with 'being an alien, to whom leave to land had been refused, was found in the UK'. Being in the UK was enough to make her guilty.

4. **A consequence** – in murder there may be a stabbing, but there must also be the consequence of death resulting from that stab wound; or, for example, a broken nose for the consequence of actual bodily harm in s47 Offences against the Person Act 1861; if the assault did not cause any injury then there is no s47 offence.

## 2.2 VOLUNTARY CONDUCT

1. The act or omission must be voluntary on the part of the defendant.

2. If the defendant has no control over his actions then he has not committed the *actus reus*.

3. In *Hill v Baxter* (1958) the court gave examples where a driver of a vehicle could not be said to be to doing the act of driving voluntarily. These included where a driver lost control of his vehicle because he:

   - was stung by a swarm of bees; or
   - was struck on the head by a stone; or
   - had a heart attack while driving.

4. Other examples of involuntary conduct include:

   - another person pushing the defendant so that the defendant falls on to the victim;
   - a reflex action;
   - a muscle spasm.

5. If the defendant knew that he was liable to lose control of his movements because of an existing health problem, then his actions would be considered as voluntary (*Broome v Perkins* (1987)).

6. Where the defendant's act occurs while he is asleep or his consciousness is impaired, or it is because of a reflex, spasm or convulsion, the defendant may have the defence of automatism. (See Chapter 8.)

## 2.3 LIABILITY FOR OMISSIONS

1. At common law there are five situations where there is a duty to act and a failure to act (omission) creates liability.

2. Acts of Parliament can create liability for an omission.

### 2.3.1 Omissions as actus reus of common law offences

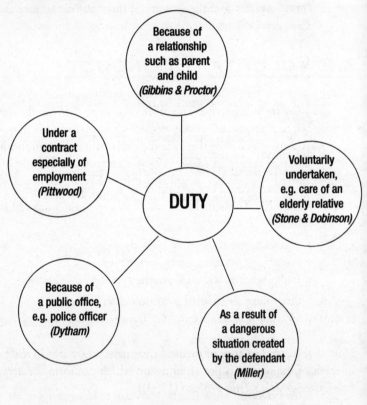

For common law crimes an omission is only sufficient for the *actus reus* where there is a duty to act. This can be:

- A contractual duty; in *Pittwood* (1902) a railway crossing keeper omitted to shut the gates so that a person crossing the line was struck and killed by a train. The keeper was guilty of manslaughter.

- A duty by virtue of a relationship, usually parent and child; in *Gibbins and Proctor* (1918) a child's father and his mistress failed to feed the child, so that it died of starvation; they were guilty of murder.
- A duty by virtue of voluntarily undertaking it; in *Stone and Dobinson* (1977) the defendants had undertaken the care of Stone's elderly sister; they were guilty of manslaughter in failing to care for her or summon help when she became helpless.
- A duty through one's official position; in *Dytham* (1979) a police officer witnessed a violent attack on the victim, but took no steps to intervene or summon help, instead he drove away from the scene. The officer was guilty of wilfully and without reasonable excuse neglecting to perform his duty.
- A duty which arises because the defendant has set in motion a chain of events; in *Miller* (1983) a squatter accidentally started a fire. When he realised this he left the room and did not attempt to put out the fire or summon help. He was guilty of arson.

Note that in *DPP v Santana-Bermudez* (2003) it was held the defendant's failure to tell a police woman, who was going to search his pockets, that he had a hypodermic needle in one of them could amount to the *actus reus* for the purposes of an assault causing actual bodily harm when she was injured by the needle.

Note that discontinuance of medical treatment where it is in the best interests of the patient is not an omission which can form the *actus reus* (*Airedale NHS Trust v Bland* (1993)).

## 2.3.2 Omissions as actus reus for statutory crimes

1. Where an offence is defined in an Act of Parliament or statutory instrument the wording determines whether it can be committed by omission.

2. Failing to report a road traffic accident is a clear example of a statutory offence of omission.
3. Wording of other offences is not always so clear; for example, s17 of the Theft Act 1968 where the offence is committed if the defendant '… destroys, defaces, conceals or falsifies any … document made or required for any accountancy purpose' has been held to be an offence of omission (*Shama* (1990)).
4. A recently created offence which can be committed by omission is causing or allowing the death of a child or vulnerable adult (s5 Domestic Violence and Victims Act 2004).

## 2.4 CAUSATION

Where a consequence must be proved, then the prosecution has to show that the defendant's conduct was:

- the factual cause of that consequence; and
- the legal cause of that consequence; and
- that there was no intervening act which broke the chain of causation.

### 2.4.1 Factual cause

The consequence would not have happened 'but for' the defendant's conduct. In *White* (1910) the defendant put cyanide in his mother's drink intending to kill her. She died of a heart attack before she could drink it. The defendant did not cause her death; he was not guilty of murder, though he was guilty of attempted murder.

### 2.4.2 Legal cause

1. The defendant's conduct must be more than a 'minimal' cause of the consequence (*Cato* (1976)).
2. But it need not be a substantial cause.
3. The defendant's conduct need not be the only cause, another's act may have contributed to the consequence.

## 2.4.3 Intervening act

1. The chain of causation can be broken by:

   - an act of a third party;
   - the victim's own act;
   - a natural but unpredictable event.

2. In order to break the chain of causation so that the defendant is not responsible for the consequence, the intervening act must be sufficiently independent of the defendant's conduct and sufficiently serious.

3. Where the defendant's conduct causes foreseeable action by a third party, then the defendant is likely to be held to have caused the consequence (*Pagett* (1983)).

4. Preparing an injection for V to self-inject does not break the chain of causation (*Kennedy* (2005)). Both D and V are engaged in the administering of the injection.

5. Medical treatment is unlikely to break the chain of causation unless it is so independent of the defendant's acts and 'in itself so potent in causing death' that the defendant's acts are insignificant (*Cheshire* (1991), *Jordan* (1956)).

6. The defendant must take the victim as he finds him as in *Blaue* (1975) where a Jehovah's witness died because she refused a blood transfusion.

7. Switching off a life support machine does not break the chain of causation (*Malcherek* (1981)).

8. If the defendant causes the victim to react in a foreseeable way, then any injury to the victim will have been caused by the defendant (*Roberts* (1971)).

9. If the victim's reaction is unreasonable, then this may break the chain of causation (*Williams* (1992)).

# CHAPTER 3

## MENS REA

The different levels of intention are shown in the chart below.

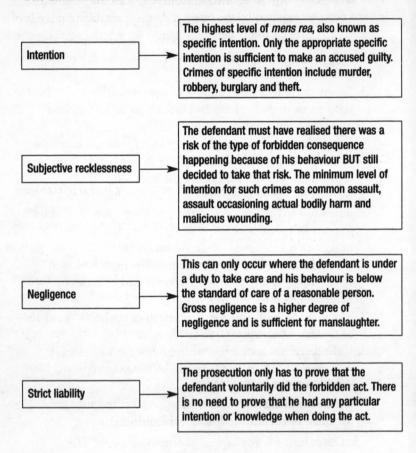

**Intention** → The highest level of *mens rea*, also known as specific intention. Only the appropriate specific intention is sufficient to make an accused guilty. Crimes of specific intention include murder, robbery, burglary and theft.

**Subjective recklessness** → The defendant must have realised there was a risk of the type of forbidden consequence happening because of his behaviour BUT still decided to take that risk. The minimum level of intention for such crimes as common assault, assault occasioning actual bodily harm and malicious wounding.

**Negligence** → This can only occur where the defendant is under a duty to take care and his behaviour is below the standard of care of a reasonable person. Gross negligence is a higher degree of negligence and is sufficient for manslaughter.

**Strict liability** → The prosecution only has to prove that the defendant voluntarily did the forbidden act. There is no need to prove that he had any particular intention or knowledge when doing the act.

# 3.1 MENTAL ELEMENT

*Mens rea* means the mental element of an offence. Each offence has its own *mens rea*. The prosecution must prove that the accused had the relevant mens rea for the offence charged. There are different levels of *mens rea*. To be guilty the accused must have at least the minimum level of *mens rea* required by the offence. As there are different levels of *mens rea*, it is difficult to define. It is easier to say what *mens rea* is not.

1. *Mens rea* is not the same as motive.
2. It does not mean an 'evil' mind.
3. It does not require knowledge that the act was forbidden by law.

# 3.2 INTENTION

1. Intention is the highest level of *mens rea*. It is also referred to as specific intention.
2. Intention has never been defined by Parliament, but the Draft Criminal Code suggested the following definition:

   '… a person acts intentionally with respect to a result when he acts either in order to bring it about or being aware that it will occur in the ordinary course of events.'
3. One judicial definition is 'a decision to bring about, in so far as it lies within the accused's power, (the prohibited consequence), no matter whether the accused desired that consequence of his act or not' (*Mohan* (1976)).
4. Intention can be divided into:

   - direct intent;
   - oblique intent (foresight of consequences).
5. Direct intent is also known as purposive intent. The defendant has a certain aim or result in mind and intends to achieve that result.
6. Oblique intent is where the defendant has one purpose in mind but in achieving that purpose also causes other

consequences. This area of intention has caused many problems.

## 3.2.1 Oblique intent/foresight of consequences

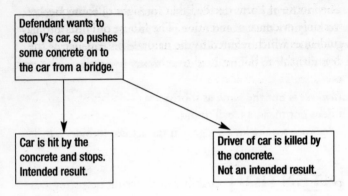

Defendant wants to stop V's car, so pushes some concrete on to the car from a bridge.

Car is hit by the concrete and stops. Intended result.

Driver of car is killed by the concrete. Not an intended result.

1. Section 8 of the Criminal Justice Act 1967 states:
   'A court or jury, in determining whether a person has committed an offence
   (a) shall not be bound in law to infer that he intended or foresaw a result of his actions by reason only of it being a natural and probable consequence of those actions; but
   (b) shall decide whether he did intend or foresee that result by referring to all the evidence, drawing such inferences from the evidence as appear proper in the circumstances.'

2. Foresight of consequences is not intention; it is only evidence from which intention can be inferred (or found) (*Moloney* (1985)).

3. Intention cannot be inferred unless the harm caused was a virtual certainty as a result of the defendant's actions and the defendant realised that this was so (*Nedrick* (1986), *Woollin* (1998)).

## 3.2.2 Key cases

1. *Moloney* (1985) – the defendant shot and killed his stepfather in a drunken challenge to see who was quicker on the draw. The House of Lords decided that foresight of consequences was only evidence of intention. The House of Lords also gave guidelines which referred to the natural consequence of the defendant's act, but omitted to mention probability. This was overruled in the next case.

2. *Hancock and Shankland* (1986) – the defendants wanted to frighten a fellow worker so that he would not break a strike by going into work. They pushed two concrete blocks from a bridge on to the road below where he was travelling to work by taxi. The taxi-driver was killed. The House of Lords pointed out that the probability of the result occurring was something to take into account in deciding whether there was sufficient evidence from which intention could be inferred.

3. *Nedrick* (1986) – the defendant poured paraffin through the letterbox of a house in order to frighten the woman who lived there. A child died in the fire. The Court of Appeal suggested that juries ask themselves two questions:

   - How probable was the consequence which resulted from the defendant's voluntary act?
   - Did the defendant foresee the consequence?

   The jury should be directed that they are not entitled to infer the necessary intention unless they feel sure that the consequence was a virtual certainty as a result of the defendant's actions and that the defendant appreciated that such was the case.

4. *Woollin* (1998) – the defendant threw his three-month-old baby towards his pram which was against a wall some three or four feet away. The baby suffered head injuries and died. The House of Lords approved the direction given in Nedrick, provided the word 'find' was used instead of 'infer'. However, the House of Lords disapproved of the use of the two questions in *Nedrick*.

# 3.3 RECKLESSNESS

1. Recklessness is the taking of an unjustifiable risk.
2. The test now is a subjective one: that is the defendant must realise the risk, but decides to take it. This is known as Cunningham recklessness.
3. Where a statute uses the word 'maliciously' to indicate the *mens rea* required, this word means doing something intentionally or being subjectively reckless about the risk involved (*Cunningham* (1957)).
4. Between 1982 and 2003 the criminal law also recognised an objective test for recklessness. This was where an ordinary prudent person would have realised the risk; the defendant could then be guilty even if he did not realise the risk. This was known as Caldwell recklessness.
5. This interpretation of recklessness in criminal damage was overruled by the House of Lords in *G and another* (2003). This case laid down that the test for recklessness in criminal damage is the subjective test.

## 3.3.1 Cunningham recklessness

1. This is subjective recklessness. The defendant realised that there was a risk of the consequence happening, but decided to take that risk.
2. In *Cunningham* (1957) the defendant tore a gas meter from the wall of an empty house in order to steal money in it. This caused gas to seep into the house next door affecting a woman there. Cunningham was not guilty of an offence against s23 of the Offences against the Person Act 1861 of maliciously administering a noxious thing, as he did not realise the risk of gas escaping into the next-door house. He had not intended to cause the harm, nor had he been subjectively reckless.
3. The case of *Savage* (1992) confirmed that *Cunningham* recklessness applies to all offences in which the statutory definition uses the word 'maliciously'.

4. For the offence of rape, the defendant must intend to have sexual intercourse, but subjective recklessness is sufficient in relation to the question of consent (*Satnam Singh* (1983)).

### 3.3.2 Caldwell recklessness

1. This was a wider test covering both subjective and objective recklessness.
2. *Caldwell* (1982), who was drunk, set fire to a hotel. The fire was put out and no serious damage was done. Caldwell was charged with arson with intent to endanger life or being reckless as to whether life was endangered. In s1(2) Criminal Damage Act 1971, the House of Lords ruled that a person was reckless if he did an act which created an obvious risk; and when he did the act he either:
   (a) had not given any thought to the possibility of there being any such risk; or
   (b) had recognised that there was some risk involved but had gone on to take the risk.
3. In *Lawrence* (1982) it was stated that, in order for the defendant to be reckless, there must be something in the circumstances that would have drawn the attention of an ordinary prudent individual to the possibility that his act might cause the consequences.
4. This test was applied to criminal damage cases until *Caldwell* was overruled by *G and another* (2003). The test of objective recklessness is no longer used in the criminal law.

## 3.4 NEGLIGENCE

1. Negligence is failing to meet the standards of the reasonable man.
2. Some statutory offences of strict liability have no-negligence defences, i.e. the defendant will be not guilty if he can prove he was not negligent.
3. Gross negligence is where the 'negligence of the accused went beyond a mere matter of compensation between subjects and

showed such disregard for the life and safety of others as to amount to a crime against the State and conduct deserving of punishment' (*Bateman* (1925)).
4. Gross negligence is one of the ways in which manslaughter can be committed (*Adomako* (1994)).

## 3.5 KNOWLEDGE

1. Some statutory offences use the word 'knowingly'. This indicates that *mens rea* is required for the offence.
2. Knowingly includes:

   - actually having knowledge of a particular fact;
   - being virtually certain that a particular fact is true;
   - being wilfully blind to the truth.

## 3.6 TRANSFERRED MALICE

1. This is the principle that the defendant is guilty if he intended to commit a similar crime but against a different victim.
2. An example is aiming a blow at one person with the necessary *mens rea* for some kind of assault. This will be sufficient to make the defendant guilty even though the blow strikes another person (*Latimer* (1886)).
3. In some cases the defendant may have no specific victim in mind, e.g. a terrorist planting a bomb in a pub. The defendant's *mens rea* is imputed so as to apply to the actual victim.
4. If the *mens rea* is for a completely different type of offence then the defendant may not be guilty (*Pembliton* (1874)).

# CHAPTER 4

## STRICT LIABILITY

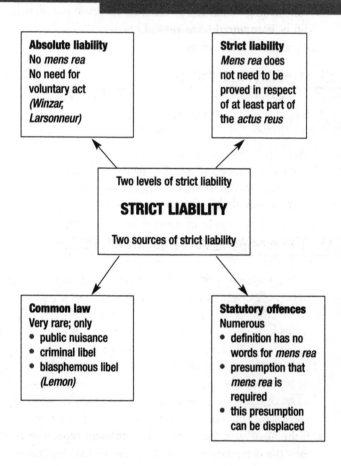

**Absolute liability**
No *mens rea*
No need for
voluntary act
*(Winzar,
Larsonneur)*

**Strict liability**
*Mens rea* does
not need to be
proved in respect
of at least part of
the *actus reus*

Two levels of strict liability

**STRICT LIABILITY**

Two sources of strict liability

**Common law**
Very rare; only
• public nuisance
• criminal libel
• blasphemous libel
  *(Lemon)*

**Statutory offences**
Numerous
• definition has no
  words for *mens rea*
• presumption that
  *mens rea* is
  required
• this presumption
  can be displaced

# 4.1 ABSOLUTE LIABILITY

1. This is very rare.
2. The offence requires no *mens rea*.
3. The defendant's *actus reus* need not be voluntary (*Winzar* (1983), *Larsonneur* (1933)).

## 4.2 STRICT LIABILITY

1. Neither *mens rea* nor negligence need be proved in respect of one or more elements of the *actus reus*.
2. The *actus reus* must be proved.
3. The defence of mistake is not available.

## 4.3 COMMON LAW STRICT LIABILITY OFFENCES

1. Strict liability is very rare in common law offences.
2. Public nuisance and criminal libel probably do not require *mens rea*, but there are no modern cases.
3. Blasphemous libel is a strict liability offence (*Lemon* (1979)).
4. Criminal contempt of court was a strict liability offence at common law. It is now a statutory offence and Parliament has continued it as a strict liability offence.

## 4.4 STATUTORY STRICT LIABILITY OFFENCES

1. About half of all statutory offences are strict liability (i.e. over 3500 offences).
2. The courts start by assuming that *mens rea* is required, but are prepared to interpret the offence as one of strict liability if Parliament has expressly or by implication indicated this in the relevant statute.
3. The modern judicial attitude is to avoid interpreting offences as strict liability (*Sweet v Parsley* (1970), *B (a minor) v DPP* (2000), *K* (2001), *Kumar* (2004)).
4. The necessary implication may be found by the courts from 'the language used, the nature of the offence, the mischief sought to be prevented and other circumstances that might assist' (Lord Nicholls in *B v DPP*).

## 4.4.1 The Gammon tests

In *Gammon (Hong Kong) Ltd v A-G of Hong Kong* (1985) the Privy Council set out five factors to be considered.

> 1. There is a presumption that *mens rea* is required before a person can be guilty of a criminal offence.
> 2. The presumption is particularly strong where the offence is 'truly criminal' in character.
> 3. The presumption applies to statutory offences and can be displaced only if this is clearly or by necessary implication the effect of the statute.
> 4. The only situation in which the presumption can be displaced is where the statute is concerned with an issue of social concern; public safety is such an issue.
> 5. Even where the statute is concerned with such an issue, the presumption of *mens rea* stands unless it can be shown that the creation of strict liability will be effective to promote the objects of the statute by encouraging greater vigilance to prevent the commission of the prohibited act.

## 4.4.2 Looking at the wording of an Act

> 1. Where words indicating *mens rea* are used, (e.g. knowingly, intentionally, maliciously or permitting) the offence requires *mens rea* and is not one of strict liability.
> 2. Where the particular offence has no words of intention, but other sections in the Act do, then it is likely that this offence is a strict liability offence (*Storkwain* (1986)).
> 3. But even this is not a conclusive test as in *Sherras v de Rutzen* (1895) where it was held that *mens rea* was still required.
> 4. Where other sections allow for a defence of no negligence but another section does not, then this indicates that it is an offence of strict liability (*Harrow London Borough Council v Shah* (1999)).
> 5. Where one section allows a defence when D reasonably believed that V was older than the relevant age for an offence,

but another section has no such defence, then the latter section may be regarded as creating strict liability (*G* (2006), where D reasonably believed that V was over 13, D was still guilty under s5 of the Sexual Offences Act 2003).

### 4.4.3 Quasi criminal offences

1. Regulatory offences which are not considered truly criminal matters are more likely to be interpreted as strict liability.
2. This includes offences such as breaches of regulations for selling food (*Callow v Tillstone* (1900)) and causing pollution (*Alphacel Ltd v Woodward* (1972)).
3. Where an offence carries a penalty of imprisonment it is less likely to be an offence of strict liability (*B v DPP* (2000)).
4. But some offences carrying imprisonment have been made strict liability offences (*Champ* (1981), *Gammon* (1985)).

## 4.5 JUSTIFICATION FOR STRICT LIABILITY

1. It protects society by:
   - promoting greater care over matters of public safety;
   - encouraging higher standards, e.g. of hygiene in processing and selling food.
2. It is easier to enforce as there is no need to prove *mens rea*.
3. It saves court time as people are more likely to plead guilty.
4. Parliament can provide a no-negligence defence where this is thought appropriate.
5. Lack of blameworthiness can be taken into account when sentencing.

### 4.5.1 Arguments against strict liability

1. Liability should not be imposed on people who are not blameworthy.

**2.** Those who have taken all possible care should not be penalised (*Harrow London Borough Council v Shah* (1999)).

**3.** There is no evidence that it improves standards.

**4.** It is contrary to the principles of human rights.

# CHAPTER 5

## PARTICIPATION

**Principal offender**
- directly causes the *actus reus*
- has *mens rea* for offence
- can have two or more joint principals (*Tyler v Whatmore*)

**Innocent agent**
Where the principal acts through another, who is not guilty, because:
- no capacity; or
- no *mens rea*; or
- has a defence (*Bourne*)

**PARTICIPATION**

**Secondary party**

*Actus reus*
- aids
- abets
- counsels
- procures

Accessories and Abettors Act 1861
(*Attorney-General's Ref* (No 1 of 1975))

*Mens rea*
Intends to assist principal
Knowledge of type of offence (*Bainbridge* (1959))
or
Contemplation of what principal might do (*Powell: English* (1997))

# 5.1 PRINCIPAL OFFENDERS

**1.** This is the person whose act is the immediate cause of the *actus reus*.

**2.** A principal offender must also have the necessary *mens rea* to be guilty of the offence.

**3.** There can be two or more joint or co-principals.

## 5.1.1 Joint principals

**1.** Where two or more people do the *actus reus* with the required *mens rea* (e.g. two burglars enter a house to steal) then they are all principals (*Tyler v Whatmore* (1976)).

**2.** Where an offence is committed by one of two people but it is not possible to prove which of them did the *actus reus*:

- if they had a joint purpose, one is the principal and the other(s) are accessories: all will be guilty of the offence (*Mohan v R* (1967), *Russell and Russell* (1987));
- if there was no joint purpose or agreement between them, then neither can be convicted (*Strudwick* (1993)).

**3.** A few offences require two or more principals for the offence to be committed, e.g. riot, affray.

# 5.2 INNOCENT AGENTS

**1.** An innocent agent is someone whom the principal uses to do the act; one who acts as a 'puppet'.

**2.** The agent may be innocent because:

- they do not have the capacity to commit the offence, e.g. where a child under the age of ten is used by an adult to enter a house and steal; or
- they do not have the necessary *mens rea* (*Cogan and Leak* (1967)); or
- they have a defence such as insanity or automatism.

# 5.3 SECONDARY PARTIES

1. A secondary party is also called an accessory.
2. A secondary party is guilty of the main crime and liable to the same punishment as the principal (s8 Accessories and Abettors Act 1861, s44 Magistrates' Courts Act 1980).
3. A secondary party can only be convicted if there was an *actus reus* for the main offence (*Thornton v Mitchell* (1940)).
   NB The Law Commission has proposed that there should be an offence of assisting or encouraging the commission of an offence, even though the offence is not actually committed (see 6.2.4).
4. A secondary party can be convicted even though the principal is acquitted, if the *actus reus* was committed, but the principal:
   - lacked the required *mens rea*; or
   - has a defence not available to the secondary party (*Bourne* (1952)).
5. If the principal has attempted the main crime then the secondary party can be guilty as an accessory to the attempt (*Donnington* (1984)).

## 5.3.1 The actus reus for secondary participation

1. The *actus reus* is that the secondary party must 'aid, abet, counsel or procure' the commission of an offence (s8, Accessories and Abettors Act 1861).
2. *Attorney-General's Reference No 1 of 1975* (1975) stated that each of these four words (aid, abet, counsel or procure) had a separate meaning.
3. Aiding is giving help, support or assistance. This can be before the offence is committed, e.g. providing tools to carry out a burglary (*Bainbridge* (1959)) or during the time it is being committed, e.g. acting as look out *(Betts and Ridley* (1930)*)*.
4. Abetting is any conduct which instigates, incites or encourages the commission of the offence.

- This can be immediately before the offence is committed or during its commission, e.g. shouting encouragement or paying for a ticket for an illegal performance (*Wilcox v Jeffery* (1951)).
- But mere presence is not usually enough for secondary participation, there must be an intention to encourage (*Clarkson* (1971), *Bland* (1988)).
- However, if there is a duty to control then passive presence may be enough (*Tuck v Robson* (1970)).

5. Counselling is advising or encouraging. It takes place before the commission of the offence (*Calhaem* (1985)).
6. Procuring means 'to produce by endeavour', that is, setting out to see that it happens and taking the appropriate steps to produce that happening (*Attorney-General's Reference No 1 of 1975* (1975)).
7. There must be a causal link between the procuring and the offence done by the principal (*Attorney-General's Reference No 1 of 1975* (1975)).

## 5.3.2 The mens rea for secondary participation

1. There must be an intention to aid, abet, counsel or procure the main offence.
2. The secondary party need only have knowledge of the type of crime and not the details of where and when, etc. (*Bainbridge* (1959)).
3. Knowledge that one of a range of offences is going to be committed may be sufficient (*Maxwell v DPP for Northern Ireland* (1979)).
4. Contemplation or foresight that the principal might commit a certain type of offence is sufficient (*Chan Wing Sui* (1985), *Powell* (1997)).
5. This rule on foresight is criticised as its effect is to put the *mens rea* for an accomplice at a lower level than that for the principal in crimes of specific intent. This can be seen as unjust, particularly in murder cases where the penalty is a mandatory life sentence for the accomplice.

**6.** Where the principal does a completely different act, then the secondary party is not liable. As in *English* (1997) where there was an agreement to assault a policeman with wooden posts, but one of the defendants killed him by stabbing him with a knife. English was not a secondary party to the murder.

### 5.3.3 Withdrawal from a joint enterprise

**1.** If the secondary party is to be not guilty, then the withdrawal from the enterprise must be clear and effective.

**2.** Repentance alone unsupported by action demonstrating withdrawal is insufficient (*Bryce* (2004)).

**3.** The more the secondary party has done towards assisting the main crime, the more effective his withdrawal must be (*Becerra* (1976), *Rook* ((1993)).

**4.** Where spontaneous violence has occurred then it is possible for the secondary party to withdraw effectively by walking away. There is no need for him to communicate his withdrawal to the principal (*Mitchell* (1998)).

## 5.4 ASSISTANCE OR CONCEALMENT AFTER A CRIME

**1.** Acts done after the crime has been committed are not done as a secondary party but may be a separate substantive offence.

**2.** The main substantive offences are :

- S4 Criminal Law Act 1967, which makes it an offence for a person who, knowing or believing that another person is guilty of an arrestable offence, does 'any act with intent to impede his apprehension or prosecution';
- S5 Criminal Law Act 1967, which makes it an offence for any person to accept money (or other bargain) in return for withholding information about an arrestable offence;
- S1 Perjury Act 1911, which makes it an offence for a witness to lie on oath in court proceedings.

# CHAPTER 6

# INCHOATE OFFENCES

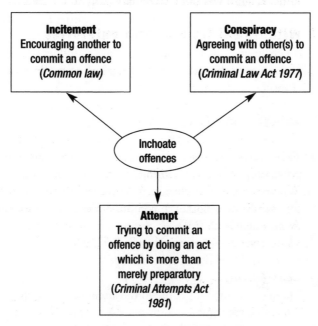

**Incitement**
Encouraging another to commit an offence (*Common law*)

**Conspiracy**
Agreeing with other(s) to commit an offence (*Criminal Law Act 1977*)

Inchoate offences

**Attempt**
Trying to commit an offence by doing an act which is more than merely preparatory (*Criminal Attempts Act 1981*)

## 6.1 INCHOATE OFFENCES

1. An inchoate offence is an incomplete offence; one which is just begun or is undeveloped. The main offence has yet to be committed.

2. There are three types of inchoate offence:
   - incitement;
   - conspiracy;
   - attempt.

3. For an inchoate offence the defendant is charged with inciting or conspiring or attempting to do the substantive crime involved. For example conspiring to murder or attempting to steal.

## 6.2 INCITEMENT

1. Incitement is a common law offence; it is not defined by an Act of Parliament. However, a few offences of incitement have their maximum penalty set out in a statute; for example incitement to murder (s4 Offences against the Person Act 1861).
2. A person who incites is one who 'seeks to influence the mind of another to the commission of a crime' (*S v Nkosiyana* (1966)).

### 6.2.1 Actus reus of incitement

1. This is anything which is aimed at encouraging, suggesting or persuading another to commit an offence (*Hendrickson and Tickner* (1977)). This can include threats or pressure used to try to influence another to commit a crime (*Race Relations Board v Applin* (1973)).
2. The incitement need not be aimed at any particular person. It can be to the whole world (*Most (1881), Invicta Plastics Ltd v Clare* (1976)).
3. The incitement must come to the attention of the incitee, i.e. it must be communicated in some way. If it is not communicated, then the inciter is guilty of an attempt to incite (*Ransford* (1874)).
4. However, the incitement does not have to succeed. The inciter can still be guilty even though the other person does not commit the substantive offence.
5. However, if the act incited is not capable of being an offence, there is no offence of incitement (*Whitehouse* (1977)).

### 6.2.2 Mens rea of incitement

1. The inciter must intend the other to commit the crime.
2. The inciter must know (or be wilfully blind to) all the circumstances which make the act incited a crime.

**3.** If the inciter believes that the person incited will not have the required *mens rea* for the substantive offence, then he is not guilty of incitement. But he may be guilty as a principal using an innocent agent (see 5.2).

**4.** There are conflicting cases on whether the person incited has to actually have the *mens rea* for the offence. As incitement may be an offence even when the person incited does not commit the crime (*Most* (1881)), this suggests that there is no need for the incitee to have the *mens rea* for the offence. However, in *Curr* (1968) it was held that the incitee had to have the *mens rea* for the offence.

## 6.2.3 Incitement and impossibility

**1.** The act which the incitement is aimed at must be capable of being an offence. If the act can never amount to an offence then the inciter is not guilty.

**2.** *Obiter dicta* in *Fitzmaurice* (1983) stated that the cases of *DPP v Nock* (1978) (common law conspiracy to do the impossible) and *Haughton v Smith* (1975) (attempting the impossible at common law) applied to incitement.

**3.** Therefore incitement to commit a factually impossible crime, such as handling stolen goods which are not in fact stolen, is not a crime.

**4.** Incitement to commit a physically impossible crime such as stealing from an empty pocket is also not a crime.

**5.** If the offence will be possible in the future then, even though it is impossible at the moment of the incitement, the inciter is guilty (*Shephard* (1919)).

**6.** If the incitement is aimed at a general crime, e.g. stealing money from someone in the street, then the offence is potentially possible and the inciter will be guilty (*Fitzmaurice* (1983)).

## 6.2.4 Proposed reform

In 2006 the Law Commission published a report recommending the creation of two new statutory inchoate offences. These would be:

- encouraging or assisting the commission of a criminal offence <u>intending</u> that the criminal act should be committed: and
- encouraging or assisting the commission of a criminal offence <u>believing</u> that encouragement or assistance will encourage or assist the commission of the criminal act and <u>believing</u> that the criminal act will be committed.

# 6.3 CONSPIRACY

1. Nearly all conspiracies are charged as statutory conspiracy under the Criminal Law Act 1977 as amended.
2. Only three types of common law conspiracy still exist (s5 Criminal Law Act 1977). These are:

- conspiracy to defraud;
- conspiracy to corrupt public morals;
- conspiracy to outrage public decency.

## 6.3.1 Statutory conspiracy

1. This is defined by s1 Criminal Law Act 1977 (as amended by s5 Criminal Attempts Act 1981) as:

'… if a person agrees with any other person or persons that a course of conduct shall be pursued which, if the agreement is carried out in accordance with their intentions, either:

(a) will necessarily amount to or involve the commission of any offence or offences by one or more of the parties to the agreement; or

(b) would do so but for the existence of facts which render the commission of the offence or any of the offences impossible, he is guilty of conspiracy to commit the offence or offences in question.'

2. The *actus reus* is the agreement of at least two persons on a course of conduct which will necessarily amount to or involve the commission of at least one offence.

3. The parties to the conspiracy need not have agreed all the details, but must have gone beyond merely talking about the possibility of committing an offence (*O'Brien* (1974)).

4. The course of conduct must necessarily 'involve the commission of an offence' (*Reed* (1982)).

5. Where there is a plan for a contingency which necessarily involves the commission of an offence, the defendant is guilty, even though the main plan may not necessarily involve the commission of an offence (*Jackson* (1985)).

6. Although it must be proved that there was an agreement between the defendant and at least one other person, the other(s) need not be identified (*Phillips* (1987)).

7. The defendant need not know all the other conspirators, provided he has agreed with one of them (*Chrastny* (1992)).

8. This means that there can be a 'chain' conspiracy where A agrees with B and B then agrees with C, but A and C do not know about each other; or there can be a 'wheel' or spoke' conspiracy where one central person agrees with several others.

**Spoke or wheel conspiracy**

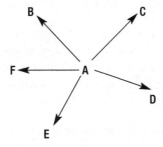

## 6.3.2 Mens rea of statutory conspiracy

1. The defendant must intend to agree to the plan; if he considers it to be a joke, then he is not agreeing to it.
2. The defendant must intend the course of conduct to be carried out and be aware that it will necessarily involve committing an offence.
3. In *Anderson* (1986) the House of Lords stated *obiter* that the *mens rea* included an intention to play some part in the agreed course of conduct. This does not accord with the wording of s1 Criminal Law Act 1977. In *Siracusa* (1989) the Court of Appeal said the House of Lords only meant that the defendant had to continue to agree to the other(s) criminal conduct.
4. In *Yip Chiu-Cheung v R* (1994) the Privy Council stressed that the necessary *mens rea* is the intention that the offence be carried out.

## 6.3.3 Conspiracy to do the impossible

1. S1(b) Criminal Law Act 1977 was inserted by s5 Criminal Attempts Act 1981.
2. This was in order to make it clear that a conspiracy to do an offence which was in fact impossible to commit was a criminal conspiracy.
3. S1(b) overturns the decision in *Nock v DPP* (1978) where it was ruled that factual or physical impossibility meant that the defendants were not guilty of conspiracy.
4. Defendants are now guilty even though there are facts which make the commission of the offence impossible, for example:

- where the items agreed to be stolen do not exist; or
- the person they agree to murder has already, unknown to them, died; or
- the substance they are planning to sell is not an illegal drug; or
- the means chosen to commit the offence will not work.

In all these situations there can now be liability for a conspiracy.

## 6.3.4 Exemption from liability for conspiracy

1. An intended victim cannot be guilty of conspiracy (s2(1) Criminal Law Act 1977).
2. Under s2(2) Criminal Law Act 1977 a person cannot be guilty if the only other person(s) he has conspired with is:
   - his/her spouse;
   - a child under the age of 10;
   - an intended victim.

## 6.3.5 Common law conspiracy

1. These are:
   - conspiracy to defraud;
   - conspiracy to corrupt public morals;
   - conspiracy to outrage public decency.
2. A defendant can be charged with both a common law conspiracy and a statutory conspiracy.
3. (a) A conspiracy to defraud is an agreement to practise a fraud on somebody.
   (b) Fraud covers conduct which may not be a substantive criminal offence (*Scott v Metropolitan Police Commissioner* (1975)).
   (c) The defendant must be dishonest (*Wai Yu-tsang* (1991)).
4. (a) Conspiracy to corrupt public morals covers conduct which would not involve the commission of an offence if carried out by one person on their own (s5(3)(b) Criminal Law Act 1977).
   (b) In *Knuller v DPP* (1972) 'corrupt' was considered as being synonymous with 'deprave' and being 'conduct which a jury might find to be destructive of the very fabric of society'.
5. (a) Conspiracy to outrage public decency also covers conduct which would not involve the commission of an offence if carried out by one person on their own (s5(3)(b) Criminal Law Act 1977).

(b) In *Knuller v DPP* (1972) 'outrage' was considered to be something which goes beyond offending or shocking reasonable people.

(c) The case of *Gibson* (1990) confirms that there is a substantive offence of outraging public decency. It can therefore be argued that a conspiracy to outrage public decency can be charged as a statutory conspiracy.

# 6.4 ATTEMPT

1. Attempting to commit an offence was made a statutory offence by the Criminal Attempts Act 1981.

2. A criminal attempt is defined by s1(1) Criminal Attempts Act 1981 as:
   'If, with intent to commit an offence …, a person does an act which is more than merely preparatory to the commission of the offence, he is guilty of attempting to commit the offence.'

3. Previous common law cases had evolved a number of tests (e.g. the last act test, the proximity test) to decide if the acts of the defendant amounted to an attempt. These tests have now been held to be irrelevant.

## 6.4.1 Actus reus of attempt

1. This is an act which is more than merely preparatory to the commission of the offence (s1(1) Criminal Attempts Act 1981).

2. More than merely preparatory means the defendant must have gone beyond purely preparatory acts and be 'embarked on the crime proper' (*Gullefer* (1987)).

3. The dividing line between merely preparatory and an attempt can explained by asking 'has the defendant done an act which shows that he has actually tried to commit the offence in question, or … has he only got ready or put himself in a position or equipped to do so?' (*Geddes* (1996)).

4. The defendant need not have performed the last act before the crime proper, nor reached the point of no return. (*A-G's reference No 1 of 1992* (1993))

5. This area between mere preparation and an attempt is difficult to define as the following cases show.

   **(a) Cases which are mere preparation**

   *Gullefer* (1987) – the defendant jumped onto a race track in order to have the race declared void and enable him to reclaim money he had bet on the race. Not guilty of attempted theft.

   *Campbell* (1990) – the defendant who had an imitation gun, sunglasses and a threatening note in his pocket was in the street outside a post office. Not guilty of attempted robbery.

   *Geddes* (1996) – the defendant was found in the boys' lavatory block of a school in possession of a large kitchen knife, some rope and masking tape. He had no right to be in the school. He had not contacted any of the pupils. Not guilty of attempted false imprisonment.

   **(b) Cases in which there was an attempt**

   *Boyle and Boyle* (1987) – the defendants were found standing by a door which had the lock and one hinge broken. Guilty of attempted burglary.

   *Jones* (1990) – the defendant had bought a shotgun, shortened the barrel, disguised himself, got into the back of the victim's car and pointed the gun at him. The gun was loaded but the safety catch was still on. Guilty of attempted murder.

## 6.4.2 Mens rea of attempt

1. The *mens rea* of an attempt is essentially that of the completed crime. The defendant has to intend to commit the substantive offence (*Easom* (1971)).

2. In some offences it is necessary to prove a higher level of *mens rea* than will suffice for the completed offence. For example, for attempted murder it is necessary to prove an intention to

kill; an intention to cause grievous bodily harm is not enough (*Whybrow* (1951)).

3. For the purposes of attempt, intention has the same meaning as at common law (*Pearman* (1984)). This means there has to be proof of a decision to bring about (the offence) no matter whether the accused desired that consequence of his act or not (*Mohan* (1976)).

4. Intention can be inferred from foresight of consequences where the consequence is virtually certain to occur a result of the defendant's actions and he is aware that this is so (*Walker and Hayles* (1990)).

5. Recklessness with regard to a consequence is not sufficient, even though it would be sufficient for the completed offence. To be guilty of an attempt the defendant must intend the consequences (*O'Toole* (1978), *Millard and Vernon* (1987)).

6. However, recklessness as to one aspect may be sufficient, such as where the defendant intends to damage property by fire and is reckless as to whether life will be endangered thereby (*A-G's reference* (No 3 of 1992) (1993)).

7. Where the defendant intends the consequence, recklessness in respect of a circumstance may be sufficient, for example, in the offence of rape regarding whether a woman is consenting to sexual intercourse (*Khan* (1990)).

## 6.4.3 Attempts to do the impossible

1. A person may be guilty of attempting to commit an offence even though the facts are such that the commission of the offence is impossible (s1(2) Criminal Attempts Act 1981).

2. If a person's intention would not be regarded as having amounted to an intent to commit an offence, but if the facts of the case had been as the defendant believed them to be, his intention would be so regarded, then he shall be regarded as having had an intent to commit that offence (s1(3) Criminal Attempts Act 1981).

3. In *Shivpuri* (1987) the House of Lords confirmed that these subsections of the Criminal Attempts Act 1981 meant that it is possible to be guilty of attempting to commit an offence even though commission of the actual offence is impossible. This overruled their earlier decision in *Anderton v Ryan* (1986).

# CHAPTER 7

# CAPACITY

**Children**
- under age of ten *doli incapax*
- ten and over fully liable for actions
  BUT
- different method of trial
- different sentencing powers

**Mentally ill**
- may be ruled unfit to plead
- if tried may be found not guilty by reason of insanity (M'Naghten Rules)
- diminished responsibility – partial defence to murder – reduces it to manslaughter

## LIMITATIONS ON CAPACITY

**Corporations**
- have legal personality so can be guilty of criminal offences
- cannot be convicted of some physical crimes, e.g. rape
- liable under one of three principles:
  identification
  vicarious liability
  breach of statutory duty

There are some circumstances in which the law rules that a person is not capable of committing a crime. The main limitations are on:
- children under the age of ten;
- mentally ill persons;
- corporations.

On the other hand there are some circumstances in which a person may be liable for the actions of another under the principle of vicarious liability.

# 7.1 CHILDREN

## 7.1.1 Children under the age of ten

1. S50 Children and Young Persons Act 1933 (as amended) states that 'it shall be conclusively presumed that no child under the age of ten can be guilty of any offence'.
2. This is known as the *doli incapax* presumption. Children under the age of 10 cannot be criminally liable for their acts.
3. This age limit is extended into quasi-criminal areas, such as anti-social behaviour orders under s1 of the Crime and Disorder Act 1998.
4. However, s11 Crime and Disorder Act 1998 allows a 'child safety order' to be made where a child under ten has committed an act which would have been an offence had he been aged ten or over.

## 7.1.2 Children aged ten and over

1. S34 Crime and Disorder Act 1998 abolished the rebuttable presumption that a child aged 10 to 13 is incapable of committing an offence.
2. This means that a child aged 10 and over is considered to be 'as responsible for his actions as if he were 40'.
3. For all but the most serious offences children (10–13) and young persons (14–17) are tried in the Youth Court.
4. Where a child or young person is being tried in the Crown Court special arrangements must be made to allow him to participate effectively in the trial. If this is not done there may be a breach of Article 6 of the European Convention on Human Rights (*T v UK; V v UK* (2000)).
5. Sentencing powers are different to those for adults.

## 7.2 MENTALLY ILL PERSONS

### 7.2.1 Unfitness to plead

1. Where, because of his mental state, the defendant is unable to understand the charge against him so as to be able to make a proper defence, he may be found unfit to plead (Criminal Procedure (Insanity) Act 1964 as amended).
2. Section 24 of the Domestic Violence, Crime and Victims Act 2004 amended the Criminal Procedure (Insanity) Act 1964, so that the decision as to whether the defendant is fit to plead is now made by a judge and not a jury.
3. If the defendant is found unfit to plead a jury must then decide whether the defendant 'did the act or made the omission charged against him'.
4. In deciding this it is not necessary for the jury to consider the mental element of the crime (*Antoine* (2000)).
5. When a defendant is found unfit to plead and that he did the act or omission, the judge has the power to make:
   - a hospital order; or
   - a supervision order (which may include a treatment requirement); or
   - an absolute discharge.

### 7.2.2 Insanity at time of offence

1. Where a person is fit to plead but is found to be insane at the time he committed the offence a special verdict of 'Not guilty by reason of insanity' is given by the jury.
2. The rules on insanity come from the M'Naghten Rules (see 8.1).
3. Where the verdict is 'Not guilty by reason of insanity', the judge has the same powers of disposal as in 7.2.1 (Criminal Procedure (Insanity and Unfitness to Plead) Act 1991).

## 7.2.3 Diminished responsibility

1. This is a partial defence which is only available on a charge of murder.
2. It operates where a person suffers from an abnormality of the mind which substantially impairs his mental responsibility for his acts or omissions in doing or being a party to the killing (s2 Homicide Act 1957) (see 9.3.1).
3. If the defence is successful the charge of murder is reduced to manslaughter.

# 7.3 CORPORATE LIABILITY

1. A corporation is a legal person (*Salomon v Salomon* (1897)). Corporations include limited companies and public corporations.
2. As a corporation is a legal person, it can be criminally liable even though it has no physical existence.
3. The Interpretation Act 1978 provides that unless the contrary intention appears, 'person' includes a corporation.
4. However, a corporation cannot be convicted of an offence where the only punishment available is physical, e.g. life imprisonment for murder.
5. A corporation cannot commit crimes of a physical nature, such as bigamy, rape or perjury, though it may be possible for a corporation to be liable as an accessory.
6. A corporation can be liable for manslaughter (*P & O European Ferries (Dover) Ltd* (1991)).
7. There are three different principles by which a corporation may be liable. These are:

   - the principle of identification;
   - vicarious liability;
   - breach of statutory duty.

## 7.3.1 The principle of identification

1. As a corporation has no physical existence it is necessary to identify those people within the corporation who can be considered as the 'directing mind and will of the company' (*HL Bolton (Engineering) v TJ Graham & Sons Ltd* (1957)).
2. The acts and intentions of those who are identified as the 'embodiment of the company' are considered the acts and intention of that company (*Tesco Supermarkets Ltd v Natrass* (1972)). Only those in senior positions can be considered as the 'controlling mind' of a corporation.
3. This is a narrow test which makes it difficult to establish corporate liability in a large company.
4. A corporation cannot be convicted of manslaughter by gross negligence if there is no evidence establishing the guilt of an identified human individual for the same crime (*A-G's Reference* (No 2 of 1999) (2000)).
5. In view of the difficulty of establishing liability, the Law Commission recommended a new offence of corporate killing.
6. In 2006, the Government placed the Corporate Manslaughter and Corporate Homicide Bill before Parliament.
7. This Bill has been criticised because the offence is only committed if the way in which corporate activities are managed or organised by its senior managers amounts to a gross breach of a relevant duty of care. This may lead to problems in identifying who are senior managers.
8. A positive aspect of the offence is that in deciding whether there has been a gross breach the jury must consider whether the evidence shows that the organisation failed to comply with health and safety legislation.
9. The jury may also consider whether the evidence shows that there were attitudes, policies, systems or accepted practices which were likely to have encouraged or tolerated breaches of health and safety legislation.

## 7.3.2 Vicarious liability

1. Corporations may be vicariously liable for the acts of their employees in the same way as a natural person.
2. For this the principles of vicarious liability set out in 7.4 apply.
3. The distinction between vicarious liability and the identification principle is that under the identification principle 'it is required that *mens rea* and *actus reus* should be established not against those who acted for or in the name of the company, but against those who were identified as the embodiment of the company' (*R v HM Coroner for East Kent, ex p Spooner* (1989)).

## 7.3.3 Breach of statutory duty

1. This occurs where a statute or regulation makes the corporation liable e.g. the Health and Safety at Work etc. Act 1974.
2. In *A-G's Reference* (No 2 of 1999) (2000), even though the company was held not guilty of manslaughter, the company pleaded guilty to a breach of statutory duty under the Health and Safety at Work etc. Act 1974.

# 7.4 VICARIOUS LIABILITY

1. The normal rule is that one person is not liable for crimes committed by another (*Huggins* (1730)).
2. However, there are some situations in which one person can be liable for the acts or omission of another. This is the principle of vicarious liability.
3. Vicarious liability for common law crimes is very rare and only occurs in offences of public nuisance and criminal libel.
4. Vicarious liability can make employers liable for the actions of their employees; principals for the actions of their agents (*Duke of Leinster* (1924)); and licensees for the actions of those to whom they delegate control of their business.
5. In statutory offences vicarious liability can exist through the extended meanings of words or under the principle of delegation.

## 7.4.1 Authorised Acts

1. Words such as 'sell' and use' are usually taken to include the employer (or principal or licensee) even though the actual sale or use is by an employee.
2. Vicarious liability has been held to exist even where the employer has taken steps to ensure that such an offence is not committed (*Coppen v Moore (No 2)* (1898)). This can only occur where an employee carries out an authorised act in an unauthorised way, as in *Coppen v Moore (No 2)* where a sales assistant sold ham which she wrongly described as 'Scotch ham' against instruction of the employer. The employer was liable because the assistant was authorised to sell the item.
3. Where the employee is not authorised to carry out the act then the employer is not liable (*Adams v Camfoni* (1929)).

## 7.4.2 Delegation principle

1. Where an offence requires proof of *mens rea* then vicarious liability can only exist if the principal has delegated responsibility.
2. In such instances the acts and intention of the person to whom responsibility has been delegated are imputed to the principal (*Allen v Whitehead* (1930)).
3. There must be complete delegation for the principal to be vicariously liable (*Vane v Yiannopoullos* (1965)).

## 7.4.3 Reasons for vicarious liability

1. It ensures that employers train and control staff properly.
2. It helps keep high standards.
3. It makes a licensee retain proper control over his business even when he is not there.
4. Without the principle of vicarious liability, it would be difficult to convict those responsible for the business.

## 7.4.4 Criticisms of vicarious liability

1. It is unjust to penalise someone for the actions of another. This is especially so where the principal has taken steps to ensure that no offence is committed (*Coppen v Moore (No 2)* (1898), *Duke of Leinster* (1929)).

2. Where an offence requires *mens rea* it is unjust to convict someone who had no knowledge of the offence.

3. The rules of vicarious liability have not been created by Parliament; they are judge-made. In some cases, e.g. where Parliament has used the word 'knowingly' in an offence, the concept of vicarious liability appears to be contrary to the intentions of Parliament.

4. There is no evidence that it helps to promote high standards.

# CHAPTER 8

# GENERAL DEFENCES

Some defences are a complete defence to all crimes. This is because the defence negates either the *mens rea* or the *actus reus* required for the offence. Other defences which are based on excusing conduct in certain circumstances are only a defence to crimes of specific intent or may not be available for certain crimes.

| Availability of different defences | | |
|---|---|---|
| **Available for all offences** | **Only available for some offences** | |
| | | Limitation |
| Insanity | Intoxication | Not available for crimes of basic intent |
| Automatism | Duress | Not available for murder, attempted murder or, possibly, treason |
| Mistake | | |
| Self-defence | Necessity | Very rarely successful as a defence |
| | Consent | Not available for murder or some assaults |

## 8.1 INSANITY

1. The rules on insanity are based on the M'Naghten Rules 1843.
2. M'Naghten had been found not guilty of murder when he tried to kill Sir Robert Peel and actually killed his secretary. The judges in the House of Lords were asked a series of questions as to what the law was in respect of insanity.
3. The first rule is that 'in all cases every man is presumed to be sane and to possess a sufficient degree of reason to be responsible for his crimes'.
4. To establish the defence of insanity the defendant must prove that at the time of committing the act, 'he was labouring

under such a defect of reason, from disease of the mind, as not to know the nature and quality of the act he was doing, or if he did know it, that he did not know he was doing what was wrong'.

5. This defence has to be established on the balance of probabilities.

6. Where a defendant is found to be insane the verdict is 'Not guilty by reason of insanity'.

7. Insanity is a defence to all crimes, except for crimes of strict liability where no mental element is required (*DPP v H* (1997)).

## 8.1.1 Defect of reason

1. The defect of reason must be more than absent-mindedness or confusion (*Clarke* (1972)).

2. It must be due to a disease which affects the mind.

## 8.1.2 Disease of the mind

1. Disease of the mind is a legal term not a medical one. The disease can be a mental disease or a physical disease which affects the mind (*Sullivan* (1984)).

2. Any mental illness which has manifested itself in violence and is prone to recur is a disease of the mind (*Bratty* (1963), *Burgess* (1991)).

3. The disease can be of any part of the body if it has an effect on the mind; for example, arteriosclerosis affecting the flow of blood to the brain (*Kemp* (1957)); or high blood sugar levels because of diabetes (*Hennessey* (1989)).

4. The disease can be one which causes a transient or intermittent impairment of reason, memory or understanding. The condition need not be permanent (*Sullivan* (1984)).

5. Where the cause is external and not a disease, then this is not insanity; for example the effect of a drug (*Quick* (1973)).

### 8.1.3 Not knowing the nature and quality of the act or not knowing that it is wrong

1. Nature and quality refers to the physical character of the act (*Codere* (1916)).
2. (a) The defendant may not know the nature and quality of the act because he is in a state of unconsciousness or impaired consciousness; or
   (b) The defendant may be conscious but not know the nature and quality of the act as due to his mental condition he does not understand or know what he is doing.
3. Where the defendant knows the nature and quality of the act he can still use the defence of insanity if he does not know that he is doing wrong. Wrong in this sense means legally wrong, not morally wrong (*Windle* (1952)).
4. Where the defendant knows the nature and quality of the act and that it is legally wrong, he cannot use the defence of insanity. This is so even where the defendant is suffering from a mental illness (*Windle* (1952)).

### 8.1.4 Reform of the law

1. Critics point out that the original statements by the judges in M'Naghten were made in 1843 when there was a very limited understanding of mental illness. The rules should be updated to reflect modern understanding.
2. Physical illnesses should not be covered by the label of 'insanity'.
3. The Butler Committee 1975 suggested that the verdict of not guilty by reason of insanity should be replaced by a verdict of not guilty on evidence of mental disorder.
4. The Draft Criminal Code suggests that a defendant should be not guilty on evidence of severe mental disorder or severe mental handicap.

# 8.2 AUTOMATISM

1. In *Bratty* (1963) automatism was defined as 'an act done by the muscles without any control by the mind, such as a spasm, a reflex action or a convulsion; or an act done by a person who is not conscious of what he is doing, such as an act done whilst suffering from concussion or whilst sleep-walking'.

2. This covers two types of automatism:

   (a) insane automatism, where the cause of the automatism is a disease of the mind within the M'Naghten rules. In such a case the defence is insanity and the verdict not guilty by reason of insanity; and

   (b) non-insane automatism where the cause is an external one. Where such a defence succeeds, it is a complete defence and the defendant is not guilty.

## 8.2.1 Non-insane automatism

1. This is a defence because the *actus reus* done by the defendant is not voluntary.

2. The cause of the automatism must be external, such as a blow from a stone or an attack by a swarm of bees (*Hill v Baxter* (1958)) or sneezing (*Whoolley* (1997)).

3. Automatism caused by external pressures such as stress does not constitute non-insane automatism, but may be insane automatism (*Burgess* (1991)).

4. However, automatism caused by an exceptional event can constitute non-insane automatism as in *R v T* (1990) where the defendant suffered post traumatic stress disorder after being raped.

5. Reduced or partial control of one's actions is not sufficient to constitute non-insane automatism. There must be 'total destruction of voluntary control' (*A–G's reference* (No 2 of 1992) (1993)).

## 8.2.2 Self-induced automatism

1. This is where the defendant knows that his conduct is likely to bring on an automatic state, for example, a diabetic failing to eat after taking insulin.
2. If the offence charged is one of specific intent, then self-induced automatism can be a defence. This is because the defendant lacks the required *mens rea* (*Bailey* (1983)).
3. If the offence charged is one of basic intent then:

a) If the defendant has been reckless in getting into a state of automatism, self-induced automatism cannot be a defence. Subjective recklessness is sufficient for the *mens rea* of crimes of basic intent (*Bailey* (1983)).

b) Similarly, where the self-induced automatic state is caused through drink or illegal drugs or other intoxicating substances the defendant cannot use the defence of automatism. Becoming voluntarily intoxicated is a reckless course of conduct (*Majewski* (1977)).

c) Where the defendant does not know that his actions are likely to lead to a self-induced automatic state in which he may commit an offence, he has not been reckless and can use the defence of automatism (*Hardie* (1984)).

## 8.3 INTOXICATION

1. This covers intoxication by alcohol, drugs or other substances, such as glue-sniffing.
2. Intoxication does not provide a defence as such, but is relevant to whether or not the defendant has the required *mens rea* for the offence. If he does not have the required *mens rea* because of his intoxicated state he may be not guilty.
3. Whether the defendant is guilty or not depends on whether the offence charged is one of specific or basic intent and whether the intoxication was voluntary or involuntary.

## 8.3.1 Voluntary intoxication

1. Voluntary intoxication can negate the *mens rea* for a specific intent offence (*Beard* (1920), *Sheehan and Moore* (1975)).
2. However, if the defendant, despite his intoxicated state, still has the necessary *mens rea*, then he is guilty of the offence. The intoxication does not provide a defence (*A-G for Northern Ireland v Gallagher* (1963)).
3. Where the offence charged is one of basic intent, intoxication is not a defence. 'It is a reckless course of conduct and recklessness is enough to constitute the necessary *mens rea*' (*Majewki* (1977), *Metropolitan Police Comr v Caldwell* (1982)).
4. However, the prosecution must prove that the defendant would have foreseen the risk had he not been intoxicated (*Richardson and Irwin* (1999)).

## 8.3.2 Involuntary intoxication

1. This covers situations where the defendant did not know he was taking an intoxicating substance; for example where a soft drink has been 'laced' with alcohol or the unexpected effect of prescribed drugs.
2. The test is, Did the defendant have the necessary *mens rea* when he committed the offence? If so, he will be guilty. The involuntary intoxication will not provide a defence (*Kingston* (1994)).
3. Even though the defendant would not have formed the *mens rea* if sober, he cannot use involuntary intoxication as a defence (*Davies* (1983)).
4. Where, however, the defendant did not have the necessary intent he will be not guilty, even if the crime is one of basic intent. This is so because in such circumstances the defendant has not been reckless (*Hardie* (1985)).

See also 8.7.1 for the effect of a drunken mistake.

|  | **Specific intent crimes** | **Basic intent crimes** |
|---|---|---|
| **Voluntary intoxication** | If defendant has *mens rea* he is guilty (*Gallagher*)<br><br>If defendant has no *mens rea* he is not guilty | Becoming intoxicated is a reckless course of conduct.<br><br>The defendant is guilty of the offence (*Majewski*) |
| **Involuntary intoxication** | If defendant has *mens rea* he is guilty (*Kingston*)<br><br>If defendant has no *mens rea* he is not guilty (*Hardie*) | The defendant has not been reckless in becoming intoxicated, so not guilty (*Hardie*) |
| **Drunken mistake** | If the mistake negates *mens rea* the defendant is not guilty<br><br>If the mistake is about the need to defend oneself it is not a defence. The defendant will be guilty | This is a reckless course of conduct, so the defendant is guilty<br><br>Exception<br>S5 Criminal Damage Act 1971 (*Jaggard v Dickinson*) |

# 8.4 DURESS

1. Duress is a defence because the defendant has been effectively forced to commit the crime. It is an excuse based on concession to human frailty. The defendant has to choose between being killed or seriously injured or committing a crime. In such a situation there is no real choice.
2. Duress can be either through a direct threat by another (duress by threats) or through external circumstances (duress of circumstances). Duress of circumstances overlaps with the defence of necessity.
3. Duress can be used as defence to all crimes, except murder (*Howe* (1987)), attempted murder (*Gotts* (1991)) and, possibly, treason (*Steane* (1947)).

## 8.4.1 Duress by threats

**1.** The threat must be of death or serious injury; lesser threats do not provide a defence (*Singh* (1971), *Valderrama-Vega* (1985)).

**2.** The threat must be to the defendant himself, or to a close member of his family. (*Ortiz* (1986)) There is no authority to say that a threat to kill an unrelated third person will provide a defence. (NB The Law Commission's Draft Criminal Code does allow for this.)

**3.** Duress can only be used as a defence if the defendant is placed in a situation where he has no safe avenue of escape. (*R v Gill* (1963)).

**4.** If the threat is not such that the defendant expects it to be carried out almost immediately, then D should take evasive action (such as going to the police) rather than commit the offence (*Hasan* (2005)).

**5.** The defence is only available if the threats to the defendant are aimed at making him commit a specific offence. Threats of violence to make the defendant repay debts did not provide a defence of duress when the defendant decided to commit a robbery in order to obtain the money (*Cole* (1994)).

**6.** The threat must be effective at the moment the crime is committed (*Hudson and Taylor* (1971)). But this does not mean that the threats need to be able to be carried out immediately (*Abdul-Hussain and others* (1999)).

**7.** There are both subjective and objective tests in deciding if the defence should succeed. This involves a two-stage test:

- was the defendant compelled to act as he did because he feared serious injury or death? (the subjective test); and
- if so, would a sober person of reasonable firmness, sharing the characteristics of the accused have responded in the same way? (the objective test) (*Graham* (1982), *Howe* (1987)).

**8.** The defendant's belief as to the elements of the threat must be reasonable and not merely genuine (*Hasan* (2005)).

**9.** Only characteristics which are relevant to the ability to resist pressure and threats can be taken into consideration. In

*Bowen* (1996) it was accepted that the following could be relevant:

- age – as very young people and the very old could be more susceptible to threats;
- pregnancy – there is the additional fear for the safety of the unborn child;
- serious physical disability – which could make it more difficult for the defendant to protect himself;
- recognised mental illness or psychiatric disorder – this could include post-traumatic stress disorder or any other disorder which meant that a person might be more susceptible to threats: this did not include a low IQ;
- sex – although the Court of Appeal thought that many women might have as much moral courage as men.

| Case on duress | Facts | Law |
| --- | --- | --- |
| *Valderama-Vega* (1985) | Smuggled cocaine because of death threats and threats to disclose homosexuality | Must be a threat of death or serious injury but can consider cumulative effect of threats |
| *Graham* (1982) | Helped kill his wife because he was threatened by his homosexual lover | Two-stage test:<br>• was D compelled to act as he did because he reasonably believed he had good cause to fear serious injury or death?<br>• if so, would a sober person of reasonable firmness, sharing the characteristics of the accused, have responded in the same way? |
| *Hasan* (2005) | D associated with a violent drug dealer. He claimed he committed a burglary because of threats | D's belief in the threat must be genuine and reasonable |

| Case on duress | Facts | Law |
|---|---|---|
| *Bowen* (1996) | Had a low IQ (68); obtained goods by deception for two men because of petrol-bomb threat | Cannot take low IQ into account<br>Can consider:<br>• age<br>• pregnancy<br>• recognised mental illness<br>• sex |
| *Gill* (1963) | Threatened so that he stole a lorry but had time to escape and raise the alarm | Cannot use duress if has a 'safe avenue of escape' |
| *Hudson and Taylor* (1971) | Two girls lied on oath because of threats to cut them up | The threat need not be capable of being carried out immediately<br><br>Take into account age and sex |
| *Abdul Hussein* (1999) | Hijacked plane to escape from persecution in Iraq | Threat must be 'imminent' and operating on D's mind when he commits the offence |

## 8.4.2 Self-induced duress

1. This may occur, for example, where a defendant has voluntarily joined a criminal gang and then been forced to commit further crimes under duress.
2. If the original crimes did not involve any violence then the defendant may use the defence of duress for the later crimes (*Shepherd* (1987)).
3. If, however, the defendant knew when he joined the gang that they were likely to use violence, duress will not be available as a defence (*Sharp* (1987)).
4. The defence of duress is not available if the defendant foresaw, or ought reasonably to have foreseen, the risk of being subjected to any compulsion by threats of violence (*Hasan* (2005)).

## 8.4.3 Duress of circumstances

1. In recent years the courts have recognised that a defendant may be forced to act by the surrounding circumstances.
2. This was shown by *Willer* (1986) when the defendant, fearing for his safety, drove on to the pavement to get away from a gang of youths. He was charged with reckless driving but the Court of Appeal said that the jury should have been allowed to consider whether the defendant drove 'under that form of compulsion, that is, under duress'.
3. In *Martin* (1989) it was decided that duress of circumstances could be available as a defence if, from an objective viewpoint, the accused acted reasonably and proportionately to avoid a threat of death or serious injury and that the same two-stage test put forward in *Graham* (1982) applied.
4. In *Pommell* (1995) the Court of Appeal said that the defence of duress of circumstances was available for all crimes except murder, attempted murder and some forms of treason.
5. In *Abdul-Hussain and others* (1999) it was stated that:
   - there must be imminent peril of death or serious injury to D, or to those for whom he has responsibility;
   - the peril must operate on D's mind at the time of committing the otherwise criminal act, so as to overbear his will; this is a matter for the jury;
   - execution of the threat need not be immediately in prospect.
6. The jury must judge the defendant on what he reasonably believes to be the situation. So a reasonable belief that a threat existed is sufficient to provide a defence, even if there was not a threat in fact (*Safi and others* (2003)).
7. In duress of circumstances the defence may be used for any offence which is an appropriate response to the danger posed by the circumstances (*Abdul-Hussein and others* (1999)).

# 8.5 NECESSITY

1. The courts have been reluctant to recognise a defence under this heading (*Dudley and Stephens* (1884)).
2. However, the defence has been implicitly recognised in some cases, especially *Bourne* (1938) and *Gillick v West Norfolk and Wisbech AHA* (1986).
3. In *Re A (Conjoined twins)* (2000) the Court of Appeal approved the following four principles of the defence of necessity, as set out in Stephen's *Digest of Criminal Law* (1883):
   (a) The act was done only in order to avoid consequences which could not otherwise be avoided.
   (b) Those consequences, if they had happened, would have inflicted inevitable and irreparable evil.
   (c) That no more was done than was reasonably necessary for that purpose.
   (d) That the evil inflicted by it was not disproportionate to the evil avoided.
4. In *Shayler* (2001) the Court of Appeal did not distinguish between duress of circumstances and necessity, but treated them as the same defence. They used similar tests to those in point 3 above:
   - the act must be done only to prevent an act of greater evil;
   - the evil must be directed towards the defendant or a person or persons for whom he was responsible;
   - the act must be reasonable and proportionate to the evil avoided.
5. This blurring of the defences of duress of circumstances and necessity can be criticised on the following points:
   (a) duress of circumstances is an excusatory defence but necessity is a defence of justification;
   (b) necessity was accepted as a defence to murder in *Re A* (2000) but duress cannot be a defence to murder.
6. Cases such as *Quayle* (2005) and *Altham* (2006) show that courts are still reluctant to allow the defence of necessity.

## 8.5.1 The role of necessity in other defences

Necessity effectively forms the basis of other defences such as:

(a) **Statutory provisions** – some Acts of Parliament set out defences based on necessity for certain crimes; these include allowing emergency vehicles a defence to breaking the speed limit 'if the observation of the limit would be likely to hinder the purpose for which the vehicle is being used'.

(b) **Self-defence** – the essence of this defence is that the defendant is claiming that he acted as he did because it was necessary for his protection.

(c) **Duress of circumstances** – as set out above, this defence, which might be considered necessity under a different title, is available for almost all crimes.

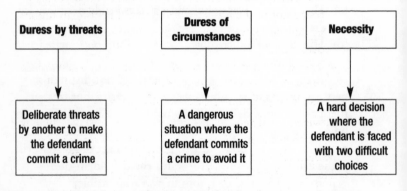

## 8.6 MARITAL COERCION

1. S47 Criminal Justice Act 1925 provides that for a wife 'it shall be a good defence to prove that the offence was committed in the presence of, and under the coercion, of the husband'.
2. The defence is not available for murder or treason.
3. The burden of proving coercion lies on the defence.
4. It is a rarely used defence, though it was used in the case of *Fitton* (2000) on a charge of drink-driving.

**5.** It can be argued that the position of wives in the twenty-first century is very different from that in 1925 and the defence should no longer be available.

# 8.7 MISTAKE

**1.** To be a defence a mistake must be a mistake about a fact, so that if the facts had been as the defendant believed them to be, it would mean:

- either there was no *mens rea* for the offence;
- or that the defendant would have been able to rely on another defence.

**2.** Simple situations will illustrate these concepts:

- if A picks up an umbrella from a stand as he is leaving a restaurant in the mistaken belief that it is his own umbrella, he does not have the *mens rea* required for theft as he is not dishonest;
- if B, in the mistaken belief that V is pointing a gun at him, throws a stone at V and knocks him out, B can plead he should be judged on the basis that his action was in self-defence.

**3.** Provided the defendant genuinely makes a mistake, there will be a defence even if the mistake is unreasonable (*DPP v Morgan* (1976), *Williams* (1987), *B v DPP* (2000)).

**4.** The defendant is judged according to his genuine mistaken view of the facts, regardless of whether his mistake was reasonable or unreasonable (*Williams* (1987)).

## 8.7.1 Drunken mistakes

**1.** If the mistake negatives the *mens rea* required for the offence then the defendant will have a defence.

**2.** If the mistake is about another aspect, for example the amount of force needed in self-defence, the defendant will not have a defence (*Lipman* (1970), *O'Grady* (1987)). *O'Grady* involved a charge of manslaughter but the case of *Hatton*

(2005) confirmed that the same rule applies on a charge of murder.

3. The law is trying to balance the needs of the defendant and the protection of victims.

4. However, in *Richardson and Irwin* (1999) the Court of Appeal held that a mistaken belief by the defendant that the victim was consenting to run the risk of personal injury would enable the defendant to avoid liability even if that mistake was induced by intoxication.

5. S5 Criminal Damage Act 1971 allows an honest belief that the person to whom the property belonged would have consented to the damage or destruction as a lawful excuse to a charge of criminal damage, whether or not the belief is justified. This has been interpreted as giving a defendant a defence even where the mistake was made through intoxication (*Jaggard v Dickinson* (1981)).

### 8.7.2 Mistake and crimes of strict liability

For these crimes, a mistake, even if reasonable, will not be a defence (*Pharmaceutical Society of Great Britain v Storkwain* (1986)).

# 8.8 SELF-DEFENCE

1. This covers not only actions needed to defend oneself from an attack, but also actions taken to defend another or prevent crime (s3 Criminal Law Act 1967).

2. The defence can be a defence to any crime, including murder, as the defendant is justifying the use of force.

3. The force used to defend oneself or another must be reasonable in the circumstances. If excessive force is used the defence will fail (*Clegg* (1994)).

4. The defendant must be judged on the facts as he believed them to be (*R v Williams* (1987)).

5. The belief need not be reasonable but the amount of force needed must be reasonable, judged objectively on the facts as the defendant believed them to be (*Owino* (1996) *DPP v Armstrong-Braun* (1999)).

6. In deciding whether the force used was reasonable, the fact that the defendant had only done what he honestly and instinctively thought was necessary in a moment of unexpected anguish is very strong evidence that the defensive action taken was reasonable (*Palmer v R* (1971)).

7. If the force is used after all danger from the assailant is over the defence of self-defence is not available.

# 8.9 CONSENT

1. Whether the victim has consented or not is an essential factor in many offences.

2. Consent is not strictly speaking a defence, because where the other person consents there is no offence. This is particularly true of sexual offences.

3. For some statutory offences, Parliament has set down an age below which a person cannot consent.

## 8.9.1 Consent and theft

1. Consent to appropriation of property does not prevent the defendant from being liable for theft (*Gomez* (1991)).

2. This is so even where the consent has not been obtained by fraud (*Hinks* (2000)).

## 8.9.2 Consent and sexual offences

1. For offences such as rape and indecent assault, consent will normally mean that the act is not unlawful and so there is no offence.

2. Girls and boys under the age of 16 cannot consent to an indecent assault (ss14(2) and 15(2) Sexual Offences Act 1956).

3. For an indecent assault (now sexual touching) where a victim only consents because they believe the defendant is medically qualified, there is no true consent. The consent is only to the nature of the act but not to its quality (*Tabassum* (2000)).

## 8.9.3 Consent and non-fatal assaults

1. Generally, the consent of the victim to an assault where there is no injury is a good defence as it prevents the act from being unlawful.
2. However, in some cases the courts have held that an unlawful act 'cannot be rendered lawful because the person to whose detriment it is done consents to it. No person can license another to commit a crime' (*Donovan* (1934)).
3. In *Attorney-General's Reference* (No 6 of 1980) (1981) where two young men agreed to fight in the street following a quarrel, the Court of Appeal held that consent could not be a defence to such an action as it was not in the public interest that people should cause each other injuries for no good reason.
4. In this case the Court of Appeal also said that consent was available as a defence to an assault in 'properly conducted games and sports, lawful chastisement or correction, reasonable surgical interference, dangerous exhibitions etc.'.
5. Although consent is not normally available as a defence where there is bodily harm, the defence may be available in contact sports (*Barnes* (2005)), particularly where the incident causing the injury is within the rules and practice of a sport.
6. The defence is not available if the conduct goes beyond what a player can reasonably be regarded as having consented to.
7. In *Brown* (1993) the House of Lords held that consent was not a defence to sado-masochistic acts, even though all the participants were adult and the injuries inflicted were transitory and trifling.
8. But in *Wilson* (1996) the Court of Appeal held that where a defendant branded his initials on his wife's buttocks with a hot knife at her request, this was not an unlawful act. It was

not in the public interest that such consensual behaviour should be criminalised.

9. Consent must be willing and informed (*Dica* (2004), *Konzani* (2005)) where the defendants were guilty of causing GBH by infecting others with HIV during consensual sex but when they had not informed the others of their HIV positive status.

## 8.9.4 Mistaken belief in consent

Where the defendant genuinely believes that the victim is consenting then there is a defence to an assault (*Jones* (1986), *Aitken* (1992), *Richardson* (1999)).

# CHAPTER 9

## HOMICIDE

Homicide is the unlawful killing of a human being. There are different offences depending on the *mens rea* of the defendant and whether there is a special defence available to the defendant.

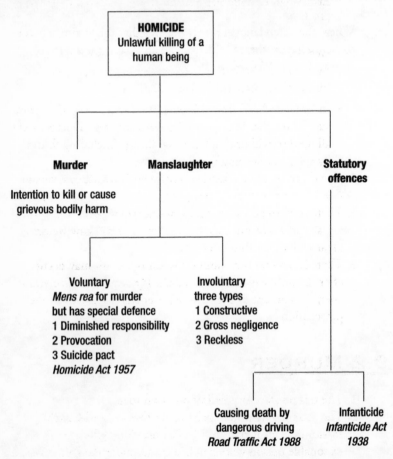

# 9.1 Actus reus of homicide

1. This is the killing of a human being (reasonable creature in being).

   - A homicide offence cannot be charged in respect of the killing of a foetus. However, if the foetus is injured and the child is born alive but dies afterwards as a result of the injuries this can be the *actus reus* for murder or manslaughter (*Attorney-General's reference* (No 3 of 1994) (1997)).

   - A person who is 'brain dead' is not considered a 'reasonable creature in being'. This is important as it allows doctors to switch off life support machines without being liable for homicide (*Malcherek and Steel* (1981)).

   - In *Airedale NHS Trust v Bland* (1993) there were *obiter dicta* statements that brain-stem death was the test. Doctors were allowed to withdraw all artificial means (including feeding by tubes) of keeping the victim alive.

2. The death must be caused by the defendant's act or omission (see 2.4 for the rules on causation).

3. There used to be a rule that death must have occurred within a year and a day, but this was abolished by the Law Reform (Year and a Day Rule) Act 1996.

4. There is now no time limit on when the death may occur after the unlawful act, but, where it is more than three years later, the consent of the Attorney-General is needed for the prosecution.

# 9.2 Murder

1. There is no statutory definition of murder.

2. The accepted definition is based on that in Lord Coke's Institutes. This is that murder is 'unlawfully killing a reasonable person who is in being and under the King's Peace with malice aforethought, express or implied.'

3. Jurisdiction over murder extends to any murder in any country by a British citizen. This means that even though the alleged offence was committed in another country the defendant may be tried for murder in an English court.

## 9.2.1 The actus reus of murder

1. See 9.1 for general rules.
2. In addition, the death can be caused by an act or by an omission (*Gibbins and Proctor* (1918)).
3. Under the King's (or Queen's) Peace means that the killing of an enemy in the course of war is not murder. However, the killing of a prisoner of war would be sufficient for the *actus reus* of murder.

## 9.2.2 The mens rea of murder

1. This is malice aforethought, express or implied. Express malice aforethought is the intention to kill. Implied malice aforethought is the intention to cause grievous bodily harm.
2. Either of these two intentions will suffice. This means that a person can be guilty of murder even though they did not intend to kill (*Vickers* (1957), *Cunningham* (1982)).
3. However, in *Attorney-General's reference* (No 3 of 1994) (1997) the House of Lords described implied malice as a 'conspicuous anomaly'.
4. Grievous bodily harm has the natural meaning of 'really serious harm' (*DPP v Smith* (1961)). However, a direction to the jury which left out the word 'really' was not considered a misdirection (*Saunders* (1985)).
5. Intention has been described as 'a decision to bring about, in so far as it lies within the accused's power, (the prohibited consequence), no matter whether the accused desired that consequence of his act or not' (*Mohan* (1976)) (see 3.2 for fuller discussion).

6. Foresight of consequences is evidence from which intention may be inferred (*Moloney* (1985)).

7. In *Woollin* (1998) it was said that the jury should be directed that they are not entitled to find the necessary intention unless they feel sure that (the consequence) was a virtual certainty as a result of the defendant's actions and that the defendant appreciated that such was the case.

## 9.2.3 Proposals for reform

1. At the end of 2006 the Law Commission published a Report (Law Com 304) on the law of murder.

2. The key proposal is that murder should be split into two degrees.

3. First degree murder would apply only where the defendant had an intention to kill or intended to do serious injury and was aware that there was a serious risk of causing death.

4. Second degree murder would include a variety of situations where D has killed V and it is more serious than involuntary manslaughter. These are:
   - where D had intended to do serious harm;
   - where D intended to cause some injury or fear or risk of injury and was aware of a serious risk of causing death;
   - where D had a partial defence through diminished responsibility, provocation or duress to what would otherwise be first degree murder.

# 9.3 VOLUNTARY MANSLAUGHTER

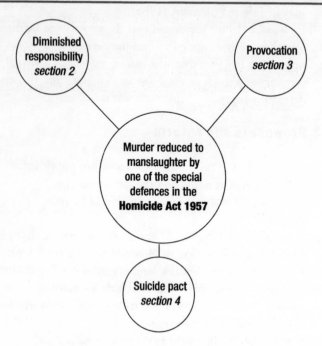

## 9.3.1 Diminished responsibility

1. 'Where a person kills or is party to a killing of another, he shall not be convicted of murder if he was suffering from such abnormality of mind … as substantially impaired his mental responsibility for his acts and omission in doing or being a party to the killing' (s2(1) Homicide Act 1957).
2. The abnormality of mind can arise from 'a condition of arrested or retarded development of mind or any inherent causes or induced by disease or injury' (s2(1) Homicide Act 1957).

## Abnormality of mind

1. There must be medical evidence of an abnormality of mind arising from one of the specified causes.
2. Abnormality of mind covers a wide range of situations. In *Byrne* (1960) it was described as 'a state of mind so different from that of ordinary human beings that the reasonable man would term it abnormal'.
3. It is wide enough to cover:
   - the perception of physical acts and matters;
   - the ability to form a rational judgment as to whether an act is right or wrong; and
   - the ability to exercise will-power to control physical acts in accordance with that rational judgment. This covers irresistible impulse (*Byrne* (1960)).
4. In *Byrne* (1960) it was said that it was 'being on the borderline of insanity'. However, in *Seers* (1984) it was held that comparisons with insanity should be avoided.
5. It has been held to cover chronic reactive depression (*Seers* (1984)); pre-menstrual tension (*Smith* (1982)); and battered wives' syndrome (*Hobson* (1997)).

## Diminished responsibility and intoxication

1. There have been problems where a defendant who pleads diminished responsibility was also intoxicated at the time of the killing.
2. In *Di Duca* (1959) the Court of Appeal held that the immediate effects of taking alcohol or drugs, even if it did have an effect on the brain, was not an injury. Such a 'transient' state of intoxication was not an abnormality of mind.
3. It was thought that the decision in *Gittens* (1984) meant that the jury had to decide whether, if the defendant had not been intoxicated, he would have killed and would have been under diminished responsibility when he did so.

4. In *Dietschmann* (2003) the House of Lords stated that this was an incorrect interpretation of *Gittens* and that:
   - the abnormality of mind and the drink might each play a part in impairing the defendant's mental responsibility for the killing;
   - the jury's task was to decide whether, despite the disinhibiting effect of the drink on the defendant's mind, the abnormality of mind nevertheless substantially impaired his mental responsibility for his fatal acts;
   - it was not correct for the judge to direct the jury that unless they were satisfied that if the defendant had not taken drink he would have killed, the defence must fail.
5. However, if the brain has been injured through alcoholism then that injury or disease can support a finding of diminished responsibility. Also where the defendant is unable to resist drinking, so that it is involuntary, this may amount to diminished responsibility (*Tandy* (1988)).

## Scope of the defence

1. The defence is available only where the defendant is charged with murder and it is only a partial defence reducing the charge of murder to manslaughter.
2. The burden of proving the defence is on the defendant (s2(2) Homicide Act 1957). But the defendant need only prove it on the balance of probabilities.

| Comparison of diminished responsibility and insanity | |
|---|---|
| Diminished responsibility | Insanity |
| Only available as a defence to murder | Available as a defence for all crimes (except, possibly, strict liability offences) |
| Verdict is not guilty of murder but guilty of manslaughter | Verdict is not guilty by reason of insanity |
| Must be an abnormality of mind | Must be a defect of reason |
| This must be due to:<br>• arrested or retarded development of mind; or<br>• any inherent causes or induced by disease or injury<br>Cause can be internal or external | This must be due to disease of the mind<br>This may be a physical or mental disease<br>The cause must be internal |
| The abnormality must substantially impair the defendant's mental responsibility | The defendant must either:<br>• not know the nature and quality of his acts; or<br>• not know he was doing wrong |
| The defence must prove diminished responsibility on the balance of probabilities | The defence must prove insanity on the balance of probabilities |

## 9.3.2 Provocation

1. 'Where, on a charge of murder, there is evidence on which the jury can find that the person charged was provoked (whether by things done or by things said or by both together) to lose his self-control, the question whether the provocation was enough to make a reasonable man do as he did shall be left to be determined by the jury' (s3 Homicide Act 1957).
2. Provocation had been a common law defence prior to the Homicide Act and the Act recognised and built on the old common law defence.

## Evidence of provocation

1. The judge decides whether there is evidence of provocation for the defence to be left to the jury (*Acott* (1997)).
2. If there is evidence which raises the possibility of provocation, the prosecution must then prove beyond reasonable doubt that the accused was not provoked (*Cascoe* (1970)).
3. Provocation can be things done or said or both. This has included the following:
   - physical assaults;
   - homosexual advances (*Newell* (1980));
   - the actions of the wife's lover in going to meet her, where the husband was provoked into killing his wife (*Davies* (1975));
   - the continual crying of a young baby (*Doughty* (1986));
4. Self-induced provocation is sufficient (*Johnson* (1989)).

## Loss of self-control

1. The defendant must lose self-control as a result of the provocation.
2. There must be 'a sudden and temporary loss of self-control, rendering the accused so subject to passion as to make him or her for the moment not master of his mind' (*Duffy* (1949)).
3. Loss of self-control does not have to be complete. It is enough that the defendant is not able to restrain himself from acting (*Richens* (1993)).
4. The longer the time lapse between the provocation and the killing, the less likely that the defence will succeed (*Ibrams* (1981), (*Thornton* (1992)).

## The reasonable man test

1. The jury must take into account the effect the provocation would have on a reasonable man (s3 Homicide Act 1957).
2. In *Camplin* (1978) it was held that age and sex and other relevant characteristics should be taken into account when considering how the reasonable man would have responded.

3. Subsequent cases tried to set down which 'other characteristics' might be relevant (*Morhall* (1995)).

4. There is a subjective test for the gravity of the provocation to the defendant. The jury must take D as they find him 'warts and all' (*A-G for Jersey v Holley* (2005)).

5. For the standard of self-control, D should be judged by the standard of a person having ordinary powers of self-control (*A-G for Jersey v Holley* (2005)). This test conflicts with one laid down by the House of Lords in *Smith (Morgan James)* (2000), which the Privy Council in *Holley* described as 'erroneous'.

6. Following the decision in *Holley* there was initially doubt as to whether the case of *Holley* or the case of *Smith (Morgan James)* should be followed. This was resolved in *James: Karimi* (2006) where it was held that the Privy Council case of *Holley* should be followed by English courts.

### 9.3.3 Suicide pact

1. 'It shall be manslaughter and shall not be murder, for a person acting in pursuance of a suicide pact between him and another to kill the other or be a party to the other being killed by a third party' (s4(1) Homicide Act 1957).

2. A suicide pact is 'a common agreement between two or more persons having for its object the death of all of them' (s4(3) Homicide Act 1957).

3. The defendant's acts will only be counted as being in pursuance of a suicide pact if 'it is done while he has the settled intention of dying in pursuance of the pact' (s4(3) Homicide Act 1957).

4. The burden of proving the defence is on the defendant (s4(2) Homicide Act 1957). But the defendant need only prove it on the balance of probabilities.

## 9.3.4 Reform of the special defences

1. In 2003 the Law Commission issued a consultation paper on the partial defences to murder.
2. This paper pointed out the problems in the defences of both diminished responsibility and provocation and put forward various ways of reforming the law.
3. One problem is the overlap of the defences of diminished responsibility and provocation following the decision in *Smith (Morgan James)* (2000).
4. A key problem in diminished responsibility is the fact that the burden of proof is on the defendant. The Law Commission suggested that this should be changed so that once the defendant raises the issue of diminished responsibility it is then for the prosecution to disprove it.
5. Another problem with diminished responsibility is that the wording of s2 of the Homicide Act is not clear. This has led to different doctors in different cases classifying the same conditions in different ways. For example, some doctors accept that reactive depressions and dissociated states of mind are inherent causes within the Act, while other doctors do not agree.
6. In 2003 the Law Commission pointed out a number of problems with the defence of provocation including that:
   - the defence as stated in section 3 of the Homicide Act 1957 contradicts itself; it raises the question of whether a reasonable man would ever respond to provocation;
   - the term reasonable man has proved difficult for the judge to explain;
   - there is no limit to the conduct which is capable of 'provoking' so that completely innocent conduct may be regarded as provocation, for example in *Doughty* (1986) when the crying of a very young baby was held to be provocation;
   - it allows a defence for anger, when there is no defence if the defendant kills in fear, despair or compassion.
7. In 2005 the Law Commission proposed that an unlawful homicide that would otherwise be murder should instead be

manslaughter if:

(a) the defendant acted in response to:

    (i) gross provocation (meaning words or conduct or a combination of words and conduct which caused the defendant to have a justifiable sense of being seriously wronged): or

    (ii) fear of serious violence towards the defendant or another; or

    (iii) a combination of (i) and (ii)

(b) a person of the defendant's age and of ordinary temperament, i.e. ordinary tolerance and self-restraint, in the circumstances of the defendant might have acted in the same or a similar way.

**8.** The Law Commission also recommended that this partial defence should not apply where:

(a) the provocation was incited by the defendant for the purpose of providing an excuse to use violence; or

(b) the defendant acted in considered desire for revenge.

# 9.4 INVOLUNTARY MANSLAUGHTER

| Involuntary manslaughter | | |
|---|---|---|
| Three different ways of committing the offence | | |
| Constructive manslaughter | Gross negligence manslaughter | Reckless manslaughter |
| Unlawful act<br><br>Objectively dangerous as to the risk of harm to the victim – *Church* (1966)<br><br>Act can be aimed at property – *Goodfellow* (1986)<br><br>Defendant must have *mens rea* for the unlawful act BUT need not realise it is dangerous – *Newbury and Jones* (1977) | Lawful act or omission<br><br>Defendant must owe victim a duty of care – *Adomako* (1994)<br><br>Act or omission must be so negligent that it 'goes beyond a matter of mere compensation' – *Bateman* (1925) | Act or omission<br><br>Subjectively reckless as to an obvious risk of injury to health – *Stone and Dobinson* (1977), *Lidar* (2000)<br><br>Possibly only exists for 'motor' manslaughter cases – *Adomako* (1994) |

## 9.4.1 Constructive manslaughter

1. The death must be caused by an unlawful act. A civil wrong is not enough (*Franklin* (1883)).
2. There have been difficulties in deciding whether there is an unlawful act where the defendant prepares an injection of a drug but the victim then injects himself. This creates difficulty also on the issue of whether the defendant has caused the death. The current law appears to be that:
   - where the defendant supplies the drug but does nothing towards the administration of it, he has not caused the death (*Dalby* (1982);
   - where the defendant assists in the injection in some way, for example by applying a tourniquet to raise the vein, he has participated in the unlawful act of administering a noxious substance and where this act causes the death he is guilty of manslaughter (*Rogers* (2003)).
   - where the defendant prepares an injection, then hands the syringe to V who self-injects and dies as a result of the drug, D is guilty of unlawful act manslaughter as he has committed the unlawful act of administering a noxious substance under s23 of the Offences against the Person Act 1861: both D and V are engaged in the 'one activity' of administering the drug (*Kennedy* (2005)).
3. There must be an act: an omission cannot not create liability for constructive manslaughter (*Lowe* (1973)).
4. The unlawful act must be dangerous on an objective test; i.e. it must be 'such as all sober and reasonable people would inevitably recognise must subject the other person to, at least, the risk of some harm resulting therefrom, albeit not serious harm' (*Church* (1966)).
5. The act need not be aimed at a person; it can be aimed at property, provided it is 'such that all sober and reasonable people would inevitably recognise must subject another person to, at least, the risk of some harm' (*Goodfellow* (1986)).

6. The risk of harm refers to physical harm; fear and apprehension are not sufficient, even if they cause the victim to have a heart attack (*Dawson* (1985)).

7. However, where a reasonable person would be aware of the victim's frailty and the risk of physical harm to him, then the defendant will be liable (*Watson* (1989)).

8. It must be proved that the defendant had the *mens rea* for the unlawful act, but it is not necessary for the defendant to realise that the act is unlawful or dangerous (*Newbury and Jones* (1977), *Attorney-General's reference* (No 2 of 1999) (2000)).

## 9.4.2 Gross negligence manslaughter

1. This is where a defendant who owes the victim a duty of care does a lawful act or omission in a very negligent way.

2. A duty of care has been held to exist for the purposes of the criminal law in various situations, including:
   - the duty of a doctor to his patient (*Adomako* (1994));
   - the duty of managing and maintaining property where there was a faulty gasfire (*Singh* (1999));
   - the duty of the owner and master of a sailing ship to the crew (*Litchfield* (1998));
   - the duty of care a lorry driver held to illegal immigrants he knew were in the back of his lorry and dependant on him to open the air vent (*Wacker* (2002)).

3. In *Khan* (1998) the Court of Appeal held that duty situations could be extended to include a duty to summon medical assistance in certain circumstances.

4. The fact that D and V were engaged on a criminal enterprise does not prevent a duty of care from arising (*Wacker* (2002), *Willoughby* (2004)).

## 9.4.3 What is gross negligence?

1. The negligence is 'gross' when it goes 'beyond a matter of mere compensation between subjects and showed such disregard for the life and safety of others as to amount to a crime against the State and conduct deserving of punishment' (*Bateman* (1925)).

2. The disregard must be as to the risk of death. Risk of injury is not enough (*Singh (Gurpal)* (1999), *Misra* (2004), *Yaqoob* (2005)).

3. In *Adomako* (1994) the House of Lords re-inforced the test from *Bateman*. Lord MacKay said the ordinary principles of negligence apply:

   - Is the defendant in breach of a duty of care?
   - Did the breach cause the death?
   - If so the jury must consider whether the breach is gross negligence and therefore a crime. This depends on the seriousness of the breach of duty in all the circumstances in which the defendant was placed.

4. Lord MacKay stated that: "the essence of the matter, which is supremely a jury question, is whether having regard to the risk of death involved, the conduct of the defendant is so bad as to amount in their judgement to a criminal act or omission."

5. The Law Commission criticised this test as being 'circular'. The jury must be directed to convict the defendant of a crime if they think his or her conduct was 'criminal'.

6. There is also the criticism that the use of the civil terminology of duty of care and negligence is unclear in the criminal law context.

7. In *Misra: Srivastava* (2004) the Court of Appeal held that the elements of gross negligence manslaughter were set out sufficiently clearly in *Adomako* (1994) so that there was no breach of Article 7 of the European Convention on Human Rights.

### 9.4.4 Reckless manslaughter

1. Prior to *Adomako* (1994) it was held that manslaughter could be committed by recklessness, based on an objective standard.
2. In *Adomako* it was stated that this was the wrong test for manslaughter, though the word 'reckless' might be appropriate. Reckless should have the meaning that the defendant had been indifferent to an obvious risk of injury to health, or actually to have foreseen the risk but determined to run it (*Stone and Dobinson* (1977)).
3. In *Lidar* (2000) the Court of Appeal approved of a direction on manslaughter by recklessness, where the risk of injury was appreciated by the defendant.
4. It is probable that reckless manslaughter only exists in 'motor' manslaughter cases (*Adomako* (1994)).

## 9.5 CAUSING DEATH BY DANGEROUS DRIVING

1. 'A person who causes the death of another by driving a mechanically propelled vehicle dangerously on a road or other public place is guilty of an offence' (s1 Road Traffic Act 1988).
2. The test for what is dangerous is an objective one. 'A person is to be regarded as driving dangerously if
   - the way he drives falls far below what would be expected of a competent and careful driver, and
   - it would be obvious to a competent and careful driver that driving in that way would be dangerous' (s2A Road Traffic Act 1988).
3. The maximum sentence is ten years' imprisonment and/or a fine.

## 9.6 INFANTICIDE

1. This is set out in the Infanticide Act 1938.
2. It is an alternative charge to the charge of murder. It is only available to a woman who has killed her child, provided the child is under the age of twelve months.
3. The woman must provide evidence that she did the killing while the balance of her mind was disturbed because she had not fully recovered from the effect of giving birth or because of breast feeding the child. It is then for the prosecution to disprove this.
4. This offence can be charged even though the mother had the *mens rea* for murder and but for the Act the offence would have amounted to murder.
5. The intention of the Act is to give the judge discretion in sentencing.

# 9.7 CAUSING OR ALLOWING THE DEATH OF A CHILD OR VULNERABLE ADULT

1. Section 5 of the Domestic Violence, Crime and Victims Act 2004 created a new offence of causing or allowing the death of a child or vulnerable adult.
2. The elements of the offence are that D:
   - was aware or ought to have been aware that V was at significant risk of serious physical harm from a member of the household; and
   - D failed to take reasonable steps to prevent that person coming to harm; and
   - the person subsequently died from the unlawful act of a member of the household in circumstances the defendant foresaw or ought to have foreseen.

# 9.8 OFFENCES AGAINST A FOETUS

Killing a foetus is not murder or manslaughter, but there are other offences which may be charged.

## 9.8.1 Child destruction

1. 'Any person who, with intent to destroy the life of a child capable of being born alive, by any wilful act causes a child to die before it has an existence independent of its mother, shall be guilty of an offence' (s1(1) Infant Life (Preservation) Act 1929).
2. Where a woman is 28 weeks or more pregnant, this is prima facie proof that the child was capable of being born alive (s1(2) Infant Life (Preservation) Act 1929).
3. However, the prosecution can try to prove that the child was capable of being born alive even though the foetus was less than 28 weeks.
4. It is not an offence if the act is done with the 'purpose of preserving the life of the mother' (*Bourne* (1939)).
5. There is no offence if the pregnancy is terminated by a registered medical practitioner in accordance with the terms of the Abortion Act 1967.

## 9.8.2 Abortion

1. Under s58 Offences against the Person Act 1861 it is an offence to try to procure a miscarriage.
2. The offence can be committed by the woman herself or by another by unlawfully administering any poison or other noxious thing or unlawfully using an instrument or any other means.
3. It is not necessary to show that a miscarriage has actually been caused.
4. Where another person is charged with the offence it is not even necessary to prove that the woman was pregnant,

provided the other acted with the intent of procuring a miscarriage.

5. By s1(1) Abortion Act 1967, there is no offence if the pregnancy is terminated by a registered medical practitioner where two doctors are of the opinion that:

- the pregnancy has not exceeded the 24th week and that the continuance of the pregnancy involves greater risk of injury to health of the woman or any existing children of her family than if the pregnancy was terminated; or
- at any time during the pregnancy if the termination is necessary to prevent grave permanent injury to the physical or mental health of the pregnant woman; or
- at any time during the pregnancy if the continuance of the pregnancy would involve greater risk to the life of the pregnant woman than if the pregnancy was terminated; or
- there is a substantial risk that if the child were born it would suffer from a serious physical or mental handicap.

# CHAPTER 10

# NON-FATAL OFFENCES AGAINST THE PERSON

| Offence | Actus reus including consequence | | Mens rea |
|---------|---------------------------------|---|----------|
| Common assault<br><br>s39 Criminal Justice Act 1988 | **Assault** – causing V to fear immediate unlawful violence<br><br>**Battery** – application of unlawful violence even the slightest touching (*Wilson v Pringle* (1986)) | No injury is required | **Assault** – intention or subjective recklessness as to causing V to fear immediate unlawful violence<br><br>**Battery** – intention of, or subjective recklessness as to applying unlawful force (*Venna* (1976)) |
| Assault occasioning actual bodily harm<br><br>s47 Offences Against the Person Act 1861 (OAPA 1861) | Assault (i.e. an assault or battery) | Actual bodily harm (e.g. bruising)<br>This includes:<br>• nervous shock (*Miller* (1954))<br>• psychiatric harm (*Chan Fook* (1994)) | Intention or subjective recklessness as to causing fear of unlawful violence or of applying unlawful force (as above) |
| Maliciously wounding or inflicting grievous bodily harm<br><br>s20 OAPA 1861 | A direct or indirect act or omission (*Martin* (1881))<br><br>No need to prove an assault (*Mandair* (1994), *Burstow* (1998)) | Either a wound (a cutting of the whole skin) (*JJC v Eisenhower* (1984))<br>**or**<br>Grievous bodily harm (really serious harm) which includes psychiatric harm (*Burstow* (1998)) | Intention or subjective recklessness as to causing some injury (though not serious) (*Savage: DPP v Parmenter* (1991)) |
| Wounding or causing grievous bodily harm with intent<br><br>s18 OAPA 1861 | A direct or indirect act or omission which causes V's injury | A wound or grievous bodily harm (as above) | Specific intention to wound or to cause grievous bodily harm or to resist or prevent arrest |

The main offences are set out in the Offences Against the Person Act 1861. This did not create a coherent set of offences and there have been many problems in the law. The Law Commission has proposed a complete reform of the law but, as yet, Parliament has not reformed the law.

The chart at the start of the chapter shows key points of four important offences against the person.

# 10.1 COMMON ASSAULT

1. There are two ways of committing this:
   - assault;
   - battery.
2. Both of these offences are charged under s39 Criminal Justice Act 1988 and are summary offences.

## 10.1.1 Assault

1. This is also known as a technical assault or a psychic assault.
2. The defendant intentionally or subjectively recklessly causes another person to fear immediate unlawful personal violence.

### Actus reus of an assault

1. An assault requires some act or words; an omission is not enough (*Fagan v Metropolitan Police Commander* (1969)).
2. Words are sufficient for an assault; even silent telephone calls can be an assault (*Ireland* (1998)).
3. Words indicating there will be no violence can prevent an act from being an assault (*Tuberville v Savage* (1669)).
4. Fear of immediate force is necessary; this does not mean instantaneous, but 'imminent', so an assault can be through a closed window (*Smith v Chief Constable of Woking* (1983)) or via a telephone call (*Ireland* (1998)).

5. Fear of any unwanted touching is sufficient: the force or unlawful personal violence which is feared need not be serious.

## Mens rea of an assault

1. The *mens rea* must be either an intention to cause another to fear immediate unlawful personal violence or recklessness as to whether such fear is caused.
2. The test for recklessness is subjective; the defendant must realise the risk that his acts/words could cause another to fear unlawful personal violence (*Venna* (1976)).

## 10.1.2 Battery

The defendant intentionally or subjectively recklessly applies unlawful force to another.

### Actus reus of battery

1. Force can include the slightest touching; but not the ordinary 'jostlings' of everyday life (*Wilson v Pringle* (1986)).
2. It may be through a continuing act (*Fagan v Metropolitan Police Commissioner* (1969)).
3. It may be through an indirect act such as a booby trap (*Martin* (1881), *DPP v K* (1990)); or causing a child to fall to the floor by punching the person holding the child (*Haystead* (2000)).
4. It has been held that a defendant's failure to tell a police woman searching his pockets that there was a hypodermic needle in one of them can amount to the *actus reus* (*DPP v Santana-Bermudez* (2003)).
5. The unlawfulness of the force may be negated by the victim's consent (see 8.9) or if it is used in self-defence (see 8.8).

### Mens rea of battery

1. The *mens rea* must be either an intention to apply unlawful physical force or recklessness.

**2.** Where recklessness is relied on, it is a subjective test, i.e. the defendant must realise the risk of physical contact and take that risk (*Venna*).

# 10.2 ASSAULT OCCASIONING ACTUAL BODILY HARM

**1.** This is an offence under s47 of the Offences against the Person Act 1861.

**2.** This states 'whosoever shall be convicted of any assault occasioning actual bodily harm shall be liable … to imprisonment for five years'.

**3.** The offence is triable either way.

## 10.2.1 Actus reus of an assault occasioning actual bodily harm

**1.** It requires a technical assault or a battery.

**2.** This must 'occasion' (cause) actual bodily harm.

**3.** Actual bodily harm is 'any hurt or injury calculated to interfere with the health or comfort' of the victim (*Miller* (1954)).

**4.** Cutting V's hair can be actual bodily harm (*Smith (Michael)* (2006)).

**5.** Psychiatric injury is sufficient, but not 'mere emotions such as fear, distress or panic' (*Chan Fook* (1994)).

## 10.2.2 Mens rea of an assault occasioning actual bodily harm

**1.** The defendant must intend or be subjectively recklessness as to whether the victim fears or is subjected to unlawful force (i.e. the *mens rea* for an assault or a battery).

**2.** There is no need for the defendant to intend or be reckless as to whether actual bodily harm is caused (*Roberts* (1971), *Savage* (1991)).

# 10.3 MALICIOUS WOUNDING/ INFLICTING GRIEVOUS BODILY HARM

1. This is an offence under s20 of the Offences against the Person Act 1861.
2. The Act states 'Whosoever shall unlawfully and maliciously wound or inflict any grievous bodily harm upon any other person, either with or without a weapon or instrument, shall be guilty of an offence'.
3. The offence is known as 'malicious wounding'.
4. The offence is triable either way and the maximum sentence is five years. This is the same as for a s47 offence, despite the fact that s20 is a more serious offence.

## 10.3.1 Actus reus of malicious wounding

1. The word 'inflict' does not require a technical assault or a battery (*Burstow* (1998)).
2. Grievous bodily harm means 'really serious harm' (*Smith* (1961)); but this does not have to be life-threatening.
3. Severe bruising may be grievous bodily harm when the victim is a very young child or frail person (*Bollom* (2004)).
4. Serious psychiatric injury can be grievous bodily harm (*Burstow*).
5. Wound means a cut or a break in the continuity of the whole skin. A cut of internal skin, such as in the cheek, is sufficient, but internal bleeding where there is no cut of the skin is not sufficient (*JCC v Eisenhower* (1984)).

## 10.3.2 Mens rea of malicious wounding

1. The defendant must intend to cause another person some harm or be subjectively reckless as to whether he suffers some harm.
2. There is no need for the defendant to foresee serious injury (*Savage* (1991), *Parmenter* (1991)).

# 10.4 WOUNDING OR CAUSING GRIEVOUS BODILY HARM WITH INTENT

1. This is an offence under s18 of the Offences against the Person Act 1861.
2. The Act states 'Whosoever shall unlawfully and maliciously by any means whatsoever wound or cause any grievous bodily harm to any person, with intent to do some grievous bodily harm to any person, or with intent to resist or prevent the lawful apprehension or detainer of any person, shall be guilty of an offence'.
3. This is an indictable offence and the maximum sentence is life imprisonment.

## 10.4.1 Actus reus of wounding or causing grievous bodily harm with intent

1. The word 'cause' is very wide so that it is only necessary to prove that the defendant's act was a substantial cause of the wound or grievous bodily harm.
2. The meanings of 'wound' and 'grievous bodily harm' are the same as for s20 (see 10.3.1 above).

## 10.4.2 Mens rea of wounding or causing grievous bodily harm with intent

1. This is a specific intent offence. The defendant must be proved to have intended to:
   - do some grievous bodily harm; or
   - resist or prevent the lawful apprehension or detainer of any person.
2. See 3.2 for explanation of intention as a concept.
3. Where the charge is intending to cause grievous bodily harm or intending to wound then, although the word 'maliciously'

appears in s18, it has been held that this adds nothing to the *mens rea* (*Mowatt* (1968)).

4. Where the charge is causing grievous bodily harm or wounding when intending to resist or prevent arrest or detention then the word 'maliciously' is important. The prosecution must prove that the defendant had specific intention to resist or prevent arrest but they need only prove that he was reckless as to whether his actions would cause a wound or injury (*Morrison* (1989)).

**Crime committed**

| Was the victim injured? | → **NO** → | Common assault and/or battery |

↓ **YES**

| How serious was that injury? | → **Slight** → | Assault occasioning actual bodily harm s47 OAPA |

↓ **Wound or really serious injury**

| Did the defendant intend to wound or cause serious harm? | → **NO** → | Malicious wounding s20 OAPA |

↓ **YES**

| Wounding with intent S18 OAPA |

# 10.5 RACIALLY AGGRAVATED ASSAULTS

1. Under s29 Crime and Disorder Act 1998, a common assault or an offence under s47 or s20 of the Offences Against the Person Act 1861 becomes a racially aggravated assault if either:

- at the time of committing the offence, or immediately before or after doing so, the offender demonstrates towards the victim of the offence hostility based on the victim's membership (or presumed membership) of a racial group; or
- the offence is motivated (wholly or partly) by hostility towards members of a racial group based on their membership of that group.

2. Where an offence is racially aggravated in this way, the maximum penalty is increased from six months to two years for common assault and from five years to seven years for both s47 and s20.

# 10.6 ADMINISTERING POISON

1. The Offences Against the Person Act 1861 creates two offences:
   - s23 'Whosoever shall unlawfully and maliciously administer to or cause to be administered to or taken by any other person any poison or other destructive or noxious thing, so as to endanger the life of such person, or so as thereby to inflict upon such person any grievous bodily harm, shall be guilty of (an offence) ...'.
   - s24 'Whosoever shall unlawfully and maliciously administer to or cause to be administered to or taken by any other person any poison or other destructive or noxious thing, with intent to injure, aggrieve, or annoy such person shall be guilty of an (offence) ...'.

2. 'Administer' has been held to include spraying with CS gas (*Gillard* (1998)).

3. For s24 a harmless substance, such as a sedative or a laxative, may become 'noxious' if administered in large quantities (*Marcus* (1981)).

4. The word 'maliciously' in both sections has the meaning given to it in *Cunningham* (1957) that the defendant must intend or be subjectively reckless about the administration of the substance.

5. S24 has an additional requirement for *mens rea* of intent to injure, aggrieve or annoy.

# CHAPTER 11

## SEXUAL OFFENCES

### Rape
s1 Sexual Offences Act 2003
- penetration of vagina, anus or mouth
- slight penetration is sufficient
- lack of consent by V
- intention to penetrate vagina, anus or mouth
- lack of reasonable belief in V's consent

Marital rape is an offence
(*R v R* (1991))

### Sexual assaults
- assault by penetration (s2)
- sexual assault (s3)

### Sexual offences on children
- rape of a child under 13 (s5)
- assault of a child under 13 by penetration (s6)
- sexual assault of a child under 13 (s7)
- sexual activity with a child under 16 (s9)

## SEXUAL OFFENCES

### Offences involving family members
- sexual activity with a child family member (s25)
- sex with an adult relative; penetration (s64)
- sex with an adult relative consenting to penetration (s65)

Forbidden relationships are parent, grandparent, brother, sister, aunt, uncle, foster parent

### Bigamy
s57 Offences Against the Person Act 1861
- going through a ceremony of marriage while married to another
- prosecution must prove first spouse is alive
- reasonable belief that first spouse is dead is a defence

# 11.1 RAPE

1. Rape is now defined by s1(1) of the Sexual Offences Act 2003 (SOA 2003).
2. A person commits rape if:
   (a) he intentionally penetrates the vagina, anus or mouth of another person with his penis;
   (b) V does not consent to the penetration; and
   (c) D does not reasonably believe that V consents.
3. Note that though the section uses the word 'person' it is clear that only a man can be the principal offender as the penetration has to be by 'his penis'. However, a woman can be guilty of rape as a secondary party.

## 11.1.1 *Actus reus* of rape

1. This consists of:
   - penetration of vagina, anus or mouth; and
   - lack of consent by V.
2. Penetration means any penetration, however slight, by D's penis.
3. Section 79 SOA 2003 states that 'penetration is a continuing act from entry to withdrawal'. This gives statutory effect to decisions in cases such as *Kaitamaki* (1985) and *Cooper and Schaub* (1994).
4. There must be absence of consent. Section 74 SOA 2003 states that a person 'consents if he agrees by choice, and has the freedom and capacity to make that choice'.
5. Section 75 makes evidential presumptions about consent. It provides that where D knows that certain circumstances exist, V is taken not to have consented. The circumstances are that at the time of the relevant act:
   - any person was using violence at the time or immediately before against V or another person or causing V to fear that immediate violence would be used against V or another person, as was the situation in *Olugboja* (1981);

- V was unlawfully detained and D was not unlawfully detained, as in *McFall* (1994) where he had kidnapped his former girlfriend at gunpoint;
- V was asleep or otherwise unconscious;
- because of physical disability, V would not have been able to communicate whether V consented;
- without V's knowledge, a person had administered to or caused V to take a substance which caused V to be stupefied or overpowered.

6. The presumption can be rebutted by proof of consent.
7. Under s76 SOA 2003 it is conclusively presumed that V did not consent in certain circumstances and that D did not believe that V had consented. The circumstances are:
   - D intentionally deceived V as to the nature or purpose of the act; this covers situations such as those in *Flattery* (1877) and *Willliams* (1923);
   - D intentionally induced V to consent to the act by impersonating a person known personally to V; this covers cases such as *Elbekkay* (1995).

## 11.1.2 *Mens rea* of rape

1. There must be an intention to penetrate V's vagina, anus or mouth.
2. There must be lack of reasonable belief in V's consent.
3. Prior to SOA 2003, it had been a defence if D honestly believed that V consented, even if that belief was not reasonable (*DPP v Morgan* (1976)).

## 11.1.3 Marital rape

1. The original view at common law was that by marrying, a woman gave consent to sexual intercourse with her husband and she could not withdraw that consent while she remained married to him. (See Hale's *History of the Pleas of the Crown* (1736).)

2. The statutory definition of rape in the Sexual Offences Act 1956 used the phrase 'unlawful sexual intercourse'. It was initially held that 'unlawful' referred to sexual intercourse outside marriage (*Chapman* (1959)).

3. However, during the second half of the twentieth century, judicial opinion gradually changed. Marital rape was recognised initially in limited situations:

- where there was a Magistrates' Court order that the wife need no longer cohabit with her husband (*Clarke* (1949));
- where there was a *decree nisi* of divorce, even though the divorce had not been finalised (*O'Brien* (1976));
- where the parties had entered into a formal separation agreement (*Roberts* (1986)).

4. Finally in *R v R* (1991) the House of Lords ruled that marital rape was an offence. They pointed out that:

- the status of women had changed;
- a modern marriage is regarded as a partnership of equals;
- the use of the word 'unlawful' meant something contrary to law rather than outside marriage.

# 11.2 ASSAULT BY PENETRATION

1. The Sexual Offences Act 2003 creates a new offence of assault by penetration (s2(1)) which is committed if the defendant:
   - intentionally penetrates the vagina or anus of another person with a part of his body or anything else, e.g. a finger as in *Coomber* (2005);
   - the penetration is sexual;
   - the other person does not consent to the penetration; and
   - the defendant does not reasonably believe that B consents.

2. This would previously have been charged as an indecent assault.

3. Section 78 of the Sexual Offences Act 2003 states that 'penetration, touching or any other activity is sexual if a reasonable person would consider that:
   (a) whatever its circumstances or any person's purpose in relation to it, it is because of its nature sexual, or
   (b) because of its nature it may be sexual and because of its circumstances or the purpose of any person in relation to it (or both) it is sexual.

## 11.3 SEXUAL ASSAULT

1. This is a new offence under s3 of the Sexual Offences Act 2003 which effectively replaces the old offence of indecent assault.
2. It is committed if:
   - the defendant intentionally touches another person;
   - the touching is sexual;
   - the victim does not consent to the touching;
   - the defendant does not reasonably believe that B consents.
3. Sexual has the meaning given in s78 of the Act (see 11.2).
4. Touching is defined in s79(8) as including touching:
   (a) with any part of the body;
   (b) with anything else;
   (c) through anything.
   There no longer needs to be an assault.
5. Touching V's clothing can be sufficient to amount to touching for purposes of s3 (*H* (2005)).
6. 'Touching amounting to penetration' is also included making a deliberate overlap between the offences in sections 2(1) and 3(1) of the Sexual Offences Act 2003.
7. Under the definition of 'sexual' in s78, certain 'touchings' are automatically 'sexual'. Whether others are depends on the circumstances and/or D's purpose.
8. 'Sexual' touching is a wide concept. The following have been accepted as 'sexual' touchings:

- touching V's breasts;
- kissing V's face;
- sniffing V's hair whilst stroking her arm.

# 11.4 RAPE AND OTHER OFFENCES AGAINST CHILDREN UNDER 13

1. S5(1) of the Sexual Offences Act 2003 creates the offence of rape of a child under 13. This is committed if:
   - the defendant penetrates the victim's vagina, anus or mouth with his penis; and
   - the victim is under 13.
2. Note that lack of consent is not an element of the *actus reus*.
3. The only *mens rea* element is that the defendant intended to penetrate the victim's vagina, anus or mouth. Liability is strict with regard to the victim's age. The defendant has no defence even if he honestly thought that the child was over 13 or over (*G* (2006)).
4. S6(1) of the Act creates the offence of assault of a child under 13 by penetration. The *actus reus* elements are that the defendant must penetrate the child's vagina or anus with a body part or anything else and the penetration must be 'sexual'. Again the only *mens rea* element stated is that the defendant intended to penetrate the child's vagina or anus. Liability is strict with regard to the child's age.
5. S7(1) of the Act creates the offence of sexual assault of a child under 13. The *actus reus* elements are that the defendant touches the child, the touching is 'sexual' and the child is under 13. Consent is irrelevant. The only *mens rea* requirement is that the defendant intended to touch the child. Liability is strict with regard to both:
   (a) the 'sexual' nature of the touching; and
   (b) the child's age.
6. A woman can be guilty of a s7(1) offence, as in *Davies* (2005) where D kissed two young girls on the lips.

# 11.5 SEXUAL ACTIVITY WITH A CHILD

1. Section 9(1) of the 2003 Act creates a new offence of 'sexual activity with a child'. This replaces the offence of unlawful sexual intercourse with a girl under 16 (s6 Sexual Offences Act 1956).
2. It is committed if the defendant is aged 18 or over and touches a child under 16. The touching must be 'sexual' (s78 SOA 2003).
3. The touching need not necessarily involve D's penis nor is it necessary that V's vagina, anus or mouth be penetrated. However, if the touching involves any of the following:
   - penetration of anus or vagina with a part of the defendant's body or anything else;
   - penetration of the mouth with the defendant's penis;
   - penetration of the defendant's anus or vagina with a part of the child's body; or
   - penetration of the defendant's mouth with the child's penis

   then the offence is indictable (s9(2)). Other touchings (not involving penetration) are triable either way (s9(3) SOA 2003).
4. If the defendant is under 18 the charge is brought under s13(1) and the maximum sentence is lower.

# 11.6 OFFENCES INVOLVING FAMILY MEMBERS

1. The Sexual Offences Act 2003 replaces the previous offence of incest with new offences of:
   - sexual activity with a child family member (s25);
   - sex with an adult relative: penetration (s64);
   - sex with an adult relative: consenting to penetration (s65).

2. An adopted child and a foster child are included in the definition of 'child family member'.
3. The relationships which can make D liable under these offences are:
   - parent;
   - grandparent;
   - brother or sister;
   - half-brother or half-sister;
   - aunt or uncle;
   - foster parents – for these it is enough if they have been the foster parent even though the fostering arrangement no longer exists.

# 11.7 OTHER CRIMES UNDER THE SEXUAL OFFENCES ACT 2003

1. The Sexual Offences Act 2003 creates a number of other offences. The main ones are given below.
2. Grooming a child by intentionally arranging or facilitating an offence under ss9–13 of the Act (s14).
3. Meeting a child, where the defendant is 18 or over and intentionally meets a child under 16 intending to commit a relevant offence (s15). This section is aimed at paedophiles who contact children on the Internet.
4. Abuse of a position of trust which involves sexual touching of a victim under the age of 18 where the defendant is in a position of trust (s16).
5. Trespass with intent to commit a sexual offence (s63). This can be committed by trespassing on any premises (not only in a building as previously in burglary with intent to rape under s9(1)(a) of the Theft Act 1968).

# 11.8 BIGAMY

1. This is an offence under s57 of the Offences against the Person Act 1861.
2. The *actus reus* of the offence is going through a ceremony of marriage while already being married to another person.
3. The prosecution must prove that the first spouse is still alive at the time of the ceremony.
4. If the first marriage has been annulled or dissolved through divorce, then no offence has been committed.
5. There is no offence where the defendant believed on reasonable grounds that the first spouse was dead (*Tolson* (1881)); or that the marriage had been dissolved. (*Gould* (1968)).

| Theft | |
|---|---|
| *Actus reus* | *Mens rea* |
| **Appropriation (s3)**<br>Any assumption of the rights of an owner<br><br>Can be appropriation even though the owner has consented to it (*Gomez* (1991), *Hinks* (2000))<br><br>If property is come by without stealing it, then any later assumption of a right to it is an appropriation (s3(1)) | **Dishonestly (s2)**<br>Two-stage test: (*Ghosh* (1982))<br>1. Was it dishonest by standards of reasonable and honest people<br>2. Did the defendant realise it was dishonest?<br>Can be dishonest even though willing to pay<br>Not dishonest if believes<br>• has right in law<br>• would have the other's consent<br>• owner of property cannot be found |
| **Property (s4)**<br>Includes money and all other property, real and personal<br>Land can only be stolen by a trustee etc.<br>Fixtures can be severed from land and stolen<br>Wild creatures cannot be stolen (s4(4))<br>Knowledge cannot be stolen (*Oxford v Moss* (1979)) | **Intention of permanently depriving (s6)**<br>Intends to treat the thing as his own regardless of the other's rights<br><br>Borrowing an item until all the goodness has gone out of it is equivalent to an outright taking (*Lloyd* (1985))<br><br>Dealing with another's property in such a manner that he knows he is risking its loss (*Fernandez* (1996)) |
| **Belonging to another (s5)**<br>Any person owning or having possession or control of the property<br>Can steal own property where another has control of it and a right over it (*Turner (No 2)* (1971)) | |

# 12.1 THEFT

1. This is an offence under s1 Theft Act 1968.
2. The Act states 'A person is guilty of theft if he dishonestly appropriates property belonging to another with the intention of permanently depriving that other of it ...'
3. The various parts of the definition are explained in sections 2 to 6 of the Act.
4. For the *actus reus* of theft three points have to be proved:

   - there was an appropriation
   - of property
   - which belonged to another.

5. For the *mens rea* of theft two points must be proved:

   - dishonesty;
   - intention to permanently deprive.

## 12.1.1 Appropriation

1. 'Any assumption by a person of the rights of an owner amounts to an appropriation' (s3(1) Theft Act 1968).
2. This includes where the person has come by the property (innocently or not) without stealing it, any later assumption of a right to it by keeping or dealing with it as an owner (s3(1) Theft Act 1968).
3. From this it can be seen that the meaning of 'appropriation' is very wide. It obviously includes physically taking property, but exercising any of the rights of an owner has been held to be an appropriation. Such rights include:

   - using;
   - selling;
   - changing price labels on goods (*Anderton v Burnside* (1983));
   - damaging or destroying (this means that there can be an overlap with criminal damage).

4. The main problem has been whether there can be theft when the owner of the property has consented to the appropriation. In *Lawrence* (1971) taking more than was due for a taxi fare from a person who did not understand English money was held to be an appropriation, even though the person held out his wallet and allowed the taxi driver to take the money.

5. In *Morris* (1983) it was stated that there had to be an element of adverse interference with or usurpation of any of the rights of the owner. The use of the word 'adverse' suggested that where the owner consented to the defendant's act, then there was no appropriation.

6. In *Gomez* (1991) goods were supplied and 'paid for' by cheques which were stolen. The shop consented to the goods being taken. It was held that this could amount to an appropriation of the goods. It did not matter that the owner had consented. The use of the word adverse in *Morris* was held to be wrong. The decision in *Gomez* creates an overlap between obtaining property by deception (s15 Theft Act 1968) and theft.

7. This was further confirmed in *Hinks* (2001) where there was no fraud in the obtaining of the consent to the transfer of the property. The word 'appropriation' was taken to be a neutral word with the meaning 'any assumption by a person of the rights of an owner' given it in s3(1) Theft Act 1968. Whether it amounted to theft would depend on whether it was done dishonestly.

## Appropriation of credit balances

The law on where and when appropriation takes places in banking cases is a little uncertain, but the principles appear to be:

- presenting a cheque – appropriation is at place and point of presentation (*Ngan* (1998));
- telex instructions – appropriation is possibly at the place of receipt of instructions or more probably at place and point of sending telex (conflicting cases of *Tomsett* (1985) and *Governor of Pentonville Prison, ex p Osman* (1989));

- computer instructions – appropriation is at place and point of receipt of instructions since operation of the keyboard produced a 'virtually instantaneous' result (*Governor of Brixton Prison, ex p Levin* (1997)).

## 12.1.2 Property

1. Property is defined as including 'money and all other property, real and personal, including things in action and other intangible property' (s4(1) Theft Act 1968).
2. Money is coins and banknotes.
3. Real property is land, but there are limitations as to when land can be stolen under s4(2) Theft Act 1968. Land can only be stolen:

   - where a trustee or personal representative or other authorised person disposes of it in 'breach of the confidence reposed in him'; or
   - when a person not in control of the land severs something from the land;
   - where a tenant misappropriates fixtures attached to the land.

4. A person who picks mushrooms, flowers, fruit or foliage growing wild does not steal what he picks unless he does it for reward or sale (s4(3) Theft Act 1968).
5. Personal property is any physical item which is not attached to land, e.g. car, boat, jewellery, furniture, paintings, etc.
6. Things in action and other intangible property includes patents, copyright, and a credit balance in a bank account.
7. The following property has been held NOT to be capable of being stolen:

   - wild creatures unless they have been tamed or kept in captivity or in another person's possession (s4(4) Theft Act 1968);
   - electricity (but there is a separate offence of dishonestly abstracting electricity (s13 Theft Act (1968));
   - information or knowledge, such as the contents of an examination paper (*Oxford v Moss* (1979)); but note that

the piece of paper on which the examination is written can be stolen;

- a corpse or part of a corpse unless they have been preserved for scientific analysis (*Kelly* (1998)).

## 12.1.3 Belonging to another

1. Property shall be regarded as belonging to any person having possession or control of it, or having in it any proprietary right (s5(1) Theft Act 1968).
2. This means that property can be stolen from people other than the owner.
3. It is even possible for a person to steal his own property if is it in control of another as in *Turner* (*No 2*) (1971) where the owner of a car was held guilty of theft of it from a garage which had done repair work on it, when he took it without informing the garage and without paying for the repairs.
4. Where property is subject to a trust, the persons to whom it belongs include any person having a right to enforce the trust (s5(2) Theft Act 1968). This allows a charge of theft to be brought against a trustee who dishonestly appropriates trust property of which he is in possession and control.
5. (a) Where a person receives property from another and is under an obligation to deal with that property in a particular way, the property shall be regarded (as against him) as belonging to the other (s5(3) Theft Act 1968).
   (b) For example, in *Davidge v Bennett* (1984) the defendant was guilty of theft when she spent money given to her by the other flat sharers to pay the gas bill.
6. (a) Where a person gets property by another's mistake, and is under an obligation to make restoration, the property shall be regarded (as against him) as belonging to the person entitled to the restoration (s5(4) Theft Act 1968).
   (b) This covers situations where money is paid into the 'wrong' bank account by mistake of the bank or where an employee is paid more then they are entitled to by their

employers. The person will only be guilty of theft if they are aware of the mistake, are being dishonest and intend to permanently deprive the other of it (*A-G's reference* (No 1 of 1983) (1985)).

## 12.1.4 Dishonestly

1. The Theft Act 1968 does not give a definition of dishonestly.
2. However, s2(1) gives three situations in which appropriation of property is not to be regarded as dishonest. These are:
   (a) where the person believes that he has in law the right to deprive the other of it;
   (b) where the person believes he would have the other's consent if the other knew of the appropriation and the circumstances of it;
   (c) where the person believes that the owner of the property cannot be discovered by taking reasonable steps.
3. A person's appropriation of property belonging to another may be dishonest even though he is willing to pay for the property (s2(2) Theft Act 1968).
4. The main case on the meaning of dishonestly is *Ghosh* (1982). This gave a two-stage test to be applied:
   - Was what was done dishonest according to the standards of reasonable and honest people? If so,
   - Did the defendant realise that what he was doing was dishonest by those standards?

## 12.1.5 Intention to permanently deprive

1. This is appropriating property and not intending to give it back. For example, taking money from an employer's till to use, but intending to replace those coins or notes with some to the same value. There is an intention to permanently deprive of the original coins and notes (*Velumyl* (1989)).
2. An intention to permanently deprive includes where the defendant does not mean the other permanently to lose the

thing, but the defendant intends 'to treat the thing as his own to dispose of regardless of the other's rights' (s6(1) Theft Act 1968).

3. A borrowing or lending of the item may amount to an intention to permanently deprive if it is 'for a period and in circumstances making it equivalent to an outright taking or disposal' (s6(1) Theft Act 1968).

4. In *Lloyd* (1985) it was held that this meant borrowing the property and keeping it until 'the goodness, the virtue, the practical value … has gone out of the article'. In this case a film had been taken for a short time and copied, then the original film replaced undamaged. Held, there was no intention to permanently deprive.

5. In *Fernandez* (1996) it was said that s6 'may apply to a person in control of another's property, who dishonestly and for his own purpose, deals with that property in such a manner that he knows he is risking its loss'.

# 12.2 ROBBERY

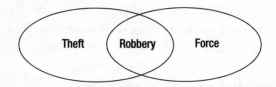

1. This is an offence under s8 of the Theft Act 1968.
2. The Act states, 'A person is guilty of robbery if he steals, and immediately before or at the time of doing so, and in order to do so, he uses force on any person or puts or seeks to put any person in fear of being then and there subjected to force'.

## 12.2.1 Actus reus of robbery

1. This is theft together with the use of force or putting someone in fear of force being used on them.

2. Where the force and the theft are quite separate from each other, this is not robbery (*Robinson* (1977)).

3. However, the act of appropriation can be a continuing one, so that any force used in order to steal while it is continuing would make this robbery (*Hale* (1978), where one accomplice tied up the householder while the other stole jewellery from rooms upstairs).

4. Only minimal force is needed (*Dawson* (1976), where the victim was 'nudged' or 'jostled' and his wallet taken as he stumbled.)

5. Wrenching property from the victim is sufficient force (*Clouden* (1987)).

## 12.2.2 Mens rea of robbery

1. There must be the *mens rea* for theft (dishonesty and an intention to permanently deprive).

2. There must also be intention to use force or subjective recklessness as to the use of force.

# 12.3 BURGLARY

| Burglary | |
|---|---|
| **Section 9(1)(a)** | **Section 9(1)(b)** |
| Enters a building or part of a building as a trespasser | Having entered a building or part of a building as a trespasser |
| with intent to:<br>• steal<br>• inflict grievous bodily harm<br>• do unlawful damage | • steals or attempts to steal; or<br>• inflicts or attempts to inflict grievous bodily harm |

1. Burglary is an offence under s9 of the Theft Act 1968.

2. There are two different ways in which burglary can be committed. These are:

(a) under s9(1)(a) he enters any building or part of a building as a trespasser and with intent to:
   - steal anything in the building;
   - inflict grievous bodily harm to any person in the building;
   - do unlawful damage to the building or anything in it;

(b) under s9(1)(b) having entered any building or part of a building as a trespasser he:
   - steals or attempts to steal anything in the building; or
   - inflicts or attempts to inflict grievous bodily harm on any person in the building.

3. These two separate offences of burglary have three elements in common:
   - entry;
   - of a building or part of a building;
   - as a trespasser.

4. The distinguishing features between the subsections are:
   - the intention at the time of entry; for s9(1)(a) the defendant must intend to do one of the three listed offences (known as ulterior offences) at the time of entering; and
   - that for s9(1)(b) the defendant must actually commit or attempt to commit one of the two listed offences; for s9(1)(a) there is no need for the ulterior offence even to be attempted.

## 12.3.1 Entry

1. In *Collins* (1973) it was held that the entry had to be 'substantial and effective'.

2. However, in *Brown* (1985) it was held that all that was required was that the entry be effective. *Brown* was standing outside the building leaning in through a window rummaging for goods.

3. Further, in *Ryan* (1996) it was held that the defendant had entered when he was part way through a window, even though he was stuck in the window.

## 12.3.2 Building or part of a building

1. A building includes an inhabited vehicle or vessel, even when there is no-one present in the vehicle or vessel (s9(4) Theft Act 1968).
2. No other definition is provided by the Theft Act 1968, but the courts have held that there must be a degree of permanence for a structure to be a building.
3. There are conflicting cases on whether a large storage container is a building.
   - In *B and S v Leathley* (1979) a 25-foot-long freezer container which had been in a yard for two years and was connected to the electricity supply was held to be a building.
   - But in *Norfolk Constabulary v Seekings and Gould* (1986) a lorry trailer with wheels was held not to be a building, even though it was connected to the electricity supply.
4. Part of building refers to situations in which the defendant may have permission to be in one part of the building (and therefore is not a trespasser in that part) but does not have permission to be in another part. Examples are storerooms in shops where shoppers would not have permission to enter or behind the counter of a shop (*Walkington* (1979)).

## 12.3.3 Trespasser

1. Where a person has permission to enter they are not a trespasser (*Collins* (1973)).
2. However, where the defendant goes beyond the permission given, he may be considered a trespasser (*Smith and Jones* (1976)).
3. The defendant must know, or be subjectively reckless, as to whether he is trespassing.

## 12.3.4 Mens rea for burglary

1. As stated above, the defendant must know, or be subjectively reckless, as to whether he is trespassing.
2. In addition, for s9(1)(a) the defendant must have the intention to commit one of the ulterior offences at the time of entering the building.
3. While for s9(1)(b) the defendant must have the *mens rea* for theft or grievous bodily harm when committing the *actus reus* of these offences.

# 12.4 AGGRAVATED BURGLARY

1. This is an offence under s10(1) Theft Act 1968.
2. The Act states that the offence is committed where the defendant commits any burglary and at the time has with him any firearm or imitation firearm, any weapon of offence, or any explosive.

   - Firearm includes an airgun or air pistol (s10(1)(a)).
   - An imitation firearm means anything which has the appearance of being a firearm, whether capable of being fired or not (s10(1)(a)).
   - Weapon of offence means any article made or adapted for use for causing injury, or intended by the person having it with him for such use (s10(1)(b)).
   - Explosive means any article manufactured for the purpose of producing a practical effect by explosion, or intended by the person having it with him for that purpose (s10(1)(c)).

3. By putting the four 'weapons' into a different order, it is easy to remember that aggravated burglary is when the burglar takes his WIFE with him!

   - Weapon of offence
   - Imitation firearm
   - Firearm
   - Explosive

### 12.4.1 'At the time has with him'

1. The defendant must have one of the four items with him at the time of the burglary. Thus for a s9(1)(a) burglary he must have it at the moment of entry, but for a s9(1)(b) burglary he must have at the point when he commits or attempts to commit the ulterior offence.
2. Where this is so, the defendant is guilty of aggravated burglary, even though he does not use the item.
3. The defendant must know he has the item 'with him'.
4. Where one of two defendants who commit burglary jointly has such an item, then if the other knows of it, he will also be guilty of aggravated burglary.
5. However, if an accomplice with such an item remains outside the building, the person entering will not have committed aggravated burglary (*Klass* (1998)).

## 12.5 TAKING A CONVEYANCE WITHOUT CONSENT

1. This is an offence under s12(1) Theft Act 1968.
2. The Act states that 'a person shall be guilty of an offence if, without the consent of the owner or other lawful authority, he takes any conveyance for his own or another's use or, knowing that any conveyance has been taken without such authority, drives it or allows himself to be carried in or on it.'
3. The rationale for the offence is to cover temporary use of a conveyance, since it is often difficult to prove that there was the intention to permanently deprive which is necessary for proving theft.

### 12.5.1 Meaning of conveyance

1. A conveyance is 'any conveyance constructed or adapted for the carriage of a person or persons whether by land, water or air' (s12(7)(a) Theft Act 1968).

2. However, pedal cycles are not included under a s12(1) offence. There is a separate offence under s12(5) Theft Act 1968 of taking a pedal cycle without authority.

## 12.5.2 *Actus reus* of taking a conveyance without consent

1. There are three ways in which the offence can be committed:
   - taking;
   - driving;
   - allowing oneself to be carried.

2. Taking is when a person assumes possession or control of the conveyance and intentionally causes it to move or be moved (*Bogacki* (1973)).

3. There can also be a taking where the defendant fails to return a conveyance or goes beyond the authority given to him to take it. For example, using an employer's lorry to drive friends to a pub (*McKnight v Davies* (1974)).

4. The taking, driving or allowing oneself to be carried must be without the consent of the owner (or other lawful authority). Consent obtained by fraud or force is not valid consent.

## 12.5.3 *Mens rea* of taking a conveyance without consent

1. If the defendant believes that he has lawful authority or that he would have the owner's consent if the owner knew of his actions, then he is not guilty (s12(6) Theft Act 1968).

2. Where the defendant is charged with driving or allowing himself to be carried, then he must know that the conveyance has been taken without consent or authority. 'Know' probably includes wilful blindness as to this fact.

# 12.6 AGGRAVATED VEHICLE-TAKING

1. This is an offence under s12A Theft Act 1968. This section was added to the Theft Act by the Aggravated Vehicle-Taking Act 1992.
2. The 1992 Act makes the taking of a vehicle a more serious offence than s12 in the following circumstances:

   - where the vehicle is driven dangerously (s12A(2)(a) Theft Act 1968); the test for dangerous is that 'it would be obvious to a competent and careful driver that driving in that way would be dangerous';
   - that, owing to the driving of the vehicle, an accident occurred by which injury was caused to any person (s12A(2)(b) Theft Act 1968);
   - that, owing to the driving of the vehicle, an accident occurred by which damage was caused to any property, other than the vehicle (s12A(2)(c) Theft Act 1968);
   - that damage was caused to the vehicle (s12A(2)(d) Theft Act 1968).

   For these last three situations it is not necessary to prove any fault in the driving of the defendant (*Marsh* (1997)).

# 12.7 HANDLING STOLEN GOODS

1. This is an offence under s22 Theft Act 1968
2. A person handles stolen goods if (otherwise than in the course of stealing) knowing or believing them to be stolen goods he dishonestly receives the goods, or dishonestly undertakes or assists in their retention, removal, disposal or realisation by or for the benefit of another person or he arranges to do so.
3. The goods must be stolen for the full offence of handling to be committed, but where the defendant believes the goods are stolen, there can be an attempt to handle them (*Shivpuri* (1986)).

**4.** Note that the thief cannot be charged with handling for anything done in the course of the theft. The correct charge against him is theft.

## 12.7.1 *Actus reus* of handling

**1.** The section creates a number of ways in which the *actus reus* may be committed:
- receiving stolen goods (taking possession or control);
- undertaking or assisting or arranging their
  - (a) retention (keeping possession of, not losing, continuing to have – *Pitchley* (1972))
  - (b) removal (transporting or carrying)
  - (c) disposal (destroying, giving them away, melting down silver, etc.);
- undertaking their realisation (selling them).

Note the last four can be by another person or by the defendant for another's benefit.

**2.** These different ways appear to cover all possible ways of unlawfully dealing with stolen goods.

## 12.7.2 *Mens rea* of handling

**1.** The defendant must know or believe the goods to be stolen.

**2.** 'Know' is where the handler has first hand information about the fact the goods are stolen, e.g. he has been told by the thief that this is so.

**3.** 'Believe' is the state of mind where the defendant says to himself 'I cannot say I know for certain that these goods are stolen, but there can be no other reasonable conclusion in the light of all the circumstances' (*Hall* (1985)).

**4.** Mere suspicion that the goods might be stolen is not enough (*Grainge* (1974)).

**5.** The handling must be done dishonestly. The test for dishonest is the same as for theft (see 12.1.4).

# 12.8 GOING EQUIPPED FOR STEALING

1. This is an offence under s25 Theft Act 1968.
2. 'A person shall be guilty of an offence if, when not at his place of abode, he has with him any article for use in the course of or in connection with any burglary, theft or cheat' (s25(1) Theft Act 1968).
3. Proof that a person had with him any article made or adapted for use in committing a burglary, theft or cheat shall be evidence that he had it with him for such use (s25(3) Theft Act 1968).
4. Where the item has an innocent use, then it is for the prosecution to prove that the defendant intended to use it for a burglary, theft or cheat.
5. In *Doukas* (1978) a wine waiter was found guilty of this offence when he sold his own wine instead of his employer's wine to customers.

# 12.9 MAKING OFF WITHOUT PAYMENT

1. This is an offence under s3 Theft Act 1978. (Note this is a different Act from the Theft Act 1968.)
2. This makes it an offence when a person who, knowing that payment on the spot for any goods supplied or service done is required or expected from him, dishonestly makes off without having paid as required or expected and with intent to avoid payment of the amount due (s3(1) Theft Act 1978).
3. This offence was created as there were situations in which it was difficult to prove theft or obtaining by deception.
4. There must be either goods supplied or a service done which is lawful. If the supply of goods is unlawful (e.g. cigarettes to someone under 16) or the service is not legally enforceable (e.g. prostitution), then no offence has been committed (s3(3) Theft Act 1978).

5. The *mens rea* of the offence involves:

- dishonesty (this is the same test as for theft; see 12.1.4);
- knowledge that payment on the spot is required; and
- an intention to avoid payment permanently (*Allen* (1985)).

# 12.10 BLACKMAIL

1. This is an offence under s21 Theft Act 1968.
2. A person is guilty of blackmail if, with a view to gain for himself or another or with intent to cause loss to another, he makes any unwarranted demand with menaces.
3. There must be a demand. If a demand is sent through the post then the demand is made when the letter is posted (*Treacy* (1971)).
4. The demand must be made with menaces. Menaces has been held to be a serious threat. This threat can be of violence or any action detrimental or unpleasant to the victim (*Thorne v Motor Trade Association* (1937)).
5. The threat must either be:

- 'of such a nature and extent that the mind of an ordinary person of normal stability and courage might be influenced or made apprehensive by it' (*Clear* (1968); in which case it is not necessary to prove that the victim was actually intimidated; or
- one which actually intimidated the victim; but if that threat was such as would not affect a normal person, the prosecution must prove that the defendant was aware of the likely effect on the victim (*Garwood* (1987)).

6. The demand must be unwarranted. A demand with menaces is unwarranted unless the person making it does so in the belief:

- that he has reasonable grounds for making the demand; and
- that the use of menaces is a proper means of reinforcing the demand (s21(1) Theft Act 1968).

7. The defendant must make the demand with a view to gain for himself. This need not be a monetary gain. In *Bevans* (1987) a demand for a morphine injection was held to be both a gain for the defendant and a loss to the doctor from whom it was demanded.

# CHAPTER 13

# DECEPTION OFFENCES

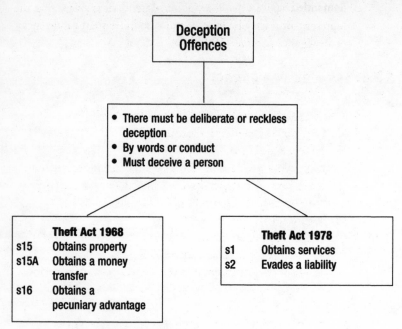

**Deception Offences**

- There must be deliberate or reckless deception
- By words or conduct
- Must deceive a person

**Theft Act 1968**
| | |
|---|---|
| s15 | Obtains property |
| s15A | Obtains a money transfer |
| s16 | Obtains a pecuniary advantage |

**Theft Act 1978**
| | |
|---|---|
| s1 | Obtains services |
| s2 | Evades a liability |

## 13.1 DECEPTION

1. All the offences covered in this chapter require a deception.
2. Deception is defined in s15(4) Theft Act 1968 as 'any deception (whether deliberate or reckless) by words or conduct as to fact or as to law, including a deception as to the present intentions of the person using the deception or any other person'.
3. A person must be deceived. If they are not, then the full offence is not committed but the defendant may be liable for an attempt.
4. It is not possible for there to be a deception of a machine, e.g. by typing in someone's PIN to obtain cash or using a foreign coin. However, this could be theft.

## 13.1.1 Deliberate or reckless

1. A deliberate deception is where the defendant knows that what he is representing is false.
2. Reckless is a subjective test; i.e. the defendant is aware that the representation may be false. It must be more than carelessness or negligence (*Staines* (1974)).

## 13.1.2 Words or conduct

1. This covers a very wide range of activities including:
    (a) showing a false identity card;
    (b) wearing a uniform;
    (c) using a cheque card or credit card where authority to use it has been withdrawn by the bank (*Metropolitan Police Commissioner v Charles* (1977), *Lambie* (1982));
    (d) staying silent where:
        - this implies an intention to pay (*DPP v Ray* (1974))
        - circumstances have changed (*Rai* (2000))
        - the defendant is under a duty to disclose information (*Firth* (1990)).

# 13.2 OBTAINING PROPERTY BY DECEPTION

1. This is an offence under s15(1) Theft Act 1968.
2. The Act states that 'any person who by any deception dishonestly obtains property belonging to another, with the intention of permanently depriving the other of it is guilty of an offence'.
3. The main difference between this offence and theft is the use of a deception and the fact that the property must be obtained as result of the deception. However, since the judgment in *Gomez* (1992) (see 12.1.1) there is a large overlap between s15 and theft and most offences of obtaining by deception could also be charged as theft.

## 13.2.1 *Actus reus* of obtaining property by deception

1. The defendant must:
   - obtain
   - property
   - belonging to another
   - and this obtaining must be because of a deception.

2. Obtaining property means obtaining ownership, possession or control of it. (s15(2) Theft Act 1968)

3. Property has the same meaning as for theft (see 12.1.2).

4. Belonging to another has the same meaning as for theft (see 12.1.3).

5. If the obtaining is not because of a deception there is no offence under s15. For example, where the property is obtained before the deception is made (*Collis-Smith* (1971)); or where the deception is about a matter which is irrelevant to the victim (*Laverty* (1970)).

## 13.2.2 *Mens rea* of obtaining property by deception

The defendant must:

- be dishonest (the test for this is the same as for theft; see 12.1.4);
- intend to permanently deprive the other of the property (this has the same meaning as for theft; see 12.1.5);
- make the deception deliberately or be reckless as to whether they are deceiving the other (see 13.1).

# 13.3 OBTAINING A MONEY TRANSFER BY DECEPTION

1. This is an offence under s15A Theft Act 1968.

2. The Act states that a person is guilty of an offence if by any deception he dishonestly obtains a money transfer for himself or another (s15A(1) Theft Act 1968).

3. A money transfer occurs when:
   - a debit is made to one account;
   - a credit is made to another; and
   - the credit results from the debit or the debit results from the credit.

4. This section was inserted into the Theft Act 1968 by the Theft (Amendment) Act 1996 when the decision in *Preddy* (1996) that a mortgage was not property highlighted a gap in the law.

5. S15A covers all transfers made by automated or electronic transfers.

# 13.4 OBTAINING A PECUNIARY ADVANTAGE BY DECEPTION

1. This is an offence under s16 Theft Act 1968.

2. The Act states that it is an offence where a person by any deception dishonestly obtains for himself or another any pecuniary advantage.

3. Pecuniary advantage is limited to cases where the person:
   - is allowed to borrow by way of overdraft or to take out any policy of insurance or annuity contract, or obtains an improvement of the terms on which he is allowed to do so (s16(2)(b) Theft Act 1968); or
   - is given the opportunity to earn remuneration or greater remuneration in an office or employment, or to win money by betting (s16(2)(c) Theft Act 1968).

4. Employment has been held to include self-employment (*Callender* (1992)).

## 13.5 OBTAINING SERVICES BY DECEPTION

1. This is an offence under s1 Theft Act 1978.
2. Any person who by any deception dishonestly obtains services from another is guilty of an offence.
3. Obtaining services occurs where 'the other is induced to confer a benefit by doing some act, or causing or permitting some act to be done, on the understanding that the benefit has been or will be paid for' (s1(2) Theft Act 1978).
4. Services now include the making of a loan; this covers mortgages (s1(3) Theft Act 1978 which was inserted by the Theft (Amendment) Act 1996).
5. *Sofroniou* (2003) held that the addition of s1(3) also means that obtaining loans through a bank account is obtaining services.
6. The understanding that the benefit has been or will be paid need only be a common understanding, such as the common understanding that bank loans and overdrafts have to be paid for. There is no need for a specific agreement that the benefit will be paid for (*Sofroniou* (2003)).

## 13.6 EVASION OF A LIABILITY

1. This is an offence under s2 Theft Act 1978.
2. It can be committed in three ways where a person by any deception:
   - dishonestly secures the remission of the whole or any part of any existing liability to make a payment, whether his own liability or another's (s2(1)(a) Theft Act 1978); or
   - with intent to make permanent default in whole or in part on any existing liability to make a payment, or with intent to let another do so, dishonestly induces the creditor or any person claiming on behalf of the creditor to wait for

payment (whether or not the due date for payment is deferred) or to forgo payment (s2(1)(b) Theft Act 1978); or
- dishonestly obtains any exemption from or abatement of liability to make a payment (s2(1)(c) Theft Act 1978).

**3.** There is some overlap between these subsections.

**4.** Under s2(1)(c) there is no need to prove that the victim realised he was granting an abatement or exemption (*Firth* (1990)).

**5.** Section 2(1)(a) covers situations where the defendant persuades his creditor to let him off repaying all or part of his debt (*Jackson* (1983)).

**6.** Section 2(1)(b) includes where the defendant persuades the creditor to accept a cheque knowing that there is no money in the account to meet it. The defendant must also intend to make permanent default (*Turner* (1974)).

# 13.7 FRAUD ACT 2006

**1.** The Fraud Act 2006 received Royal Assent in November 2006, but the offences under it will not come into effect until ordered by the Secretary of State.

**2.** The Act repeals sections 15, 15A, 15B, 16 and 20(2) of the Theft Act 1968 and also sections 1 and 2 of the Theft Act 1978.

**3.** Four main new offences will take the place of the offences set out in the earlier sections of this chapter. These will be:
- fraud by false representation;
- fraud by failing to disclose information;
- fraud by abuse of position;
- obtaining services dishonestly.

## 13.7.1 Fraud by false representation

**1.** This is an offence under s2 of the Fraud Act 2006. It is committed if D:

    (a) dishonestly makes a false representation; and
    (b) intends, by making the representation
       (i) to make a gain for himself or another, or
      (ii) to cause loss to another or to expose another to the
         risk of loss.

**2.** A representation is false if:
    (a) it is untrue or misleading; and
    (b) the person making it knows that it is, or might be,
      untrue or misleading.

**3.** A representation means any representation as to fact or law, including making a representation as to the state of mind of the person making the representation or any other person (s2(3)).

**4.** A representation may be express or implied (s2(4)).

**5.** There is no requirement that V is deceived by the representation.

## 13.7.2 Fraud by failing to disclose information

This is an offence under s3 of the Fraud Act 2006. It is committed where a person:
    (a) dishonestly fails to disclose information to another person which he is under a legal duty to disclose; and
    (b) intends by failing to disclose the information
       (i) to make a gain for himself or another, or
      (ii) to cause loss to another or to expose another to the
        risk of loss.

## 13.7.3 Fraud by abuse of position

**1.** Under s4 of the Fraud Act 2006 this offence is committed where a person:
    (a) occupies a position in which he is expected to safeguard, or not to act against, the financial interests of another person;
    (b) dishonestly abuses that position; and

(c) intends by means of abuse of that position
  (i) to make a gain for himself or another, or
  (ii) to cause loss to another or to expose another to the risk of loss.

**2.** Subsection 4(2) states that this offence can be committed by an omission as well as by an act.

## 13.7.4 Obtaining services by deception

**1.** This is committed under s11 of the Fraud Act 2006, where D obtains services for himself or another:
  (a) by a dishonest act; and
  (b) in breach of subsection (2).

**2.** A person obtains services in breach of s11(2) if:
  (a) they are made available on the basis that payment has been or will be made for or in respect of them;
  (b) he obtains them without any payment having been made for or in respect of them or without payment having been made in full: and
  (c) when he obtains them he knows
    (i) that they are being made available on the basis described in paragraph (a), or
    (ii) that they might be, but intends that payment will not be made, or will not be made in full.

## 13.7.5 Other offences under the Fraud Act 2006

Other offences are also created. These include:
- possession etc of articles for use in frauds (s6);
- making or supplying article for use in frauds (s7);
- participating in fraudulent business carried on by sole trader (s9);
- participating in fraudulent business carried on by company etc (s10).

# CHAPTER 14

## CRIMINAL DAMAGE

**CRIMINAL DAMAGE**

**Basic offence**
- s1(1) Criminal Damage Act 1971
- without lawful excuse destroys or damages property
- includes non-permanent damage (*Roe v Kingerlee*)
- must intend to do the damage or be reckless as to it

**Endangering life**
- basic offence PLUS
- intending by the damage to endanger another's life or
- be reckless as to whether the life of another is endangered

**Defence to basic offence**
- belief in consent of owner to the damage is a defence (s5(2) Criminal Damage Act 1971)
- the belief must be honestly held
- but it is immaterial whether the belief is justified (*Jaggard v Dickinson*)

# 14.1 THE BASIC OFFENCE

**1.** This is an offence under s1(1) Criminal Damage Act 1971.

**2.** The Act makes it an offence for a person who without lawful excuse destroys or damages any property belonging to another intending to destroy or damage any such property or being reckless as to whether any such property would be destroyed or damaged.

## 14.1.1 *Actus reus* of the basic offence

**1.** The property must be destroyed or damaged.

**2.** Property is defined in s10 Criminal Damage Act 1971 as property of a tangible nature, whether real or personal, and including money.

**3.** So, land is property which can be damaged although it cannot normally be stolen.

**4.** However, intangible rights cannot be damaged, though they may be stolen.

**5.** 'Destroy' includes where the property has been made useless even though it is not completely destroyed.

**6.** 'Damage' includes non-permanent damage which can be cleaned off, e.g. water soluble paint (*Hardman v Chief Constable of Avon and Somerset Constabulary* (1986)), and mud (*Roe v Kingerlee* (1986)).

**7.** Damage includes temporary impairment of value or usefulness (*Morphitis v Salmon* (1990), *Fiak* (2005)).

**8.** However, damage was held not to include spit which landed on a policeman's uniform and could be wiped off with very little effort (*A (a juvenile) v R* (1978)).

## 14.1.2 *Mens rea* of the basic offence

**1.** The defendant must do the damage or destruction either intentionally or recklessly.

**2.** The test for recklessness is subjective, that is, did the defendant realise the risk.

3. Prior to the House of Lords' decision in *G and another* (2003) it was held that recklessness meant *Caldwell*-style recklessness, which included both subjective and objective recklessness.

4. The objective test was harsh, as shown in *Elliott v C* (1983) where the defendant was incapable of appreciating the risk but was still guilty under use of the objective test.

5. In *G and another* (2003) the House of Lords overruled the decision in *Caldwell*, because the Law Lords had 'adopted an interpretation of section 1 of the 1971 Act which was beyond the range of feasible meanings', and held that only the subjective test should be used for recklessness in criminal damage.

## 14.1.3 Section 5 defence

1. S5(2) Criminal Damage Act 1971 creates defences to the basic offence.

2. S5(2)(a) states that a person will be regarded as having a lawful excuse if at the time of the act or acts alleged to constitute the offence he believed that the person or persons whom he believed to be entitled to consent to the destruction or damage to the property in question had so consented, or would have so consented to it if he or they had known of the destruction or damage and its circumstances.

3. S5(3) states that for the purposes of section 5 it is immaterial whether a belief is justified or not if it is honestly held.

4. The combination of s5(2)(a) and S5(3) allows a defence of mistake to be used, even where the defendant makes the mistake because they are intoxicated (*Jaggard v Dickinson* (1981)).

5. S5(2)(b) states that a person will be regarded as having a lawful excuse if he destroyed or damaged or threatened to destroy or damage the property in order to protect property belonging to himself or another and he believed that the property was in need of immediate protection and that the means used were reasonable in all the circumstances.

# 14.2 ENDANGERING LIFE

1. This is an aggravated offence of criminal damage under s1(2) Criminal Damage Act 1971.
2. It is committed where a person who without lawful excuse destroys or damages any property, whether belonging to himself or another:
   (a) intending to destroy or damage any property or being reckless as to whether any property would be destroyed or damaged; and
   (b) intending by the destruction or damage to endanger the life of another or being reckless as to whether the life of another would be thereby endangered.
3. The danger to life must come from the destruction or damage, not from another source in which damage was caused (*Steer* (1988)).
4. Life does not actually have to be endangered (*Sangha* (1988)).
5. Section 1(2) applies even where the property damaged is the defendant's own.
6. The *mens rea* is intending or being reckless as to both whether property would be destroyed or damaged and as to whether life would be endangered thereby.
7. The test for recklessness is subjective in both parts. D must realise that life will be endangered (*Castle* (2004)).

# 14.3 ARSON

1. Where an offence under s1 Criminal Damage Act 1971 is committed by destroying or damaging property by fire, the offence becomes arson (s1(3) Criminal Damage Act 1971).
2. In *Miller* (1983) it was held that arson could be committed by an omission where the defendant accidentally started a fire and failed to do anything to prevent damage from that fire.

# CHAPTER 15

## PUBLIC ORDER OFFENCES

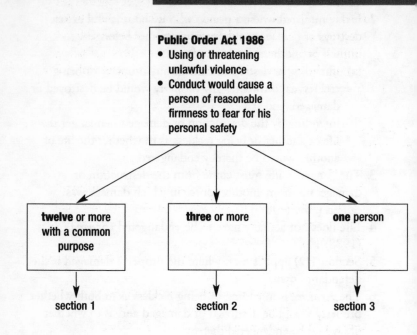

**Public Order Act 1986**
- Using or threatening unlawful violence
- Conduct would cause a person of reasonable firmness to fear for his personal safety

| **twelve** or more with a common purpose | **three** or more | **one** person |
|---|---|---|
| section 1 | section 2 | section 3 |

## 15.1 RIOT

**1.** This is an offence under s1 Public Order Act 1986.

**2.** Where twelve or more persons who are present together use or threaten unlawful violence for a common purpose and the conduct of them (taken together) is such as would cause a person of reasonable firmness present at the scene to fear for his personal safety, each of the persons using unlawful violence for the common purpose is guilty of riot.

## 15.2 VIOLENT DISORDER

1. This is an offence under s2 Public Order Act 1986.
2. Where three or more persons who are present together use or threaten unlawful violence and the conduct of them (taken together) is such as would cause a person of reasonable firmness present at the scene to fear for his personal safety, each of the persons using threatening or unlawful violence is guilty of violent disorder.

## 15.3 AFFRAY

1. This is an offence under s3 Public Order Act 1986.
2. A person is guilty of affray if he uses or threatens unlawful violence towards another and his conduct is such as would cause a person of reasonable firmness present at the scene to fear for his personal safety.
3. It is not necessary for a person of reasonable firmness to have been at the scene (*Davison* (1992)).
4. However, there must be a threat to someone who is actually present at the scene (*I, M and H v DPP* (2001));
5. Carrying dangerous weapons such as petrol bombs would amount to a threat of unlawful violence, even if they were not waved or brandished (*I, M and H v DPP* (2001)).

## 15.4 FEAR OR PROVOCATION OF VIOLENCE

1. This is an offence under s4 Public Order Act 1986.
2. A person is guilty of this offence if he:

   (a) uses towards another person threatening, abusive or insulting words or behaviour; or
   (b) distributes or displays to another any writing, sign or other visible representation which is threatening, abusive or

insulting, with intent to cause that person to believe that immediate unlawful violence will be used against him or another by any person, or to provoke the immediate use of unlawful violence by that person or another, or whereby that person is likely to believe that such violence will be used or it is likely that such violence will be provoked.

**3.** The words 'threatening, abusive or insulting words or behaviour' are not defined in the Act.

# 15.5 HARASSMENT OFFENCES

## 15.5.1 Intentional harassment, alarm or distress

**1.** This is an offence under s4A Public Order Act 1986.

**2.** A person commits this offence if, with intent to cause a person harassment, alarm or distress, he:

    (a) uses threatening, abusive or insulting words or behaviour, or disorderly behaviour, or

    (b) displays any writing, sign or other visible representation which is threatening, abusive or insulting, thereby causing that or another person harassment, alarm or distress.

## 15.5.2 Harassment, alarm or distress

**1.** This is an offence under s5 Public Order Act 1986.

**2.** A person commits this offence if he:

    (a) uses threatening, abusive or insulting words or behaviour, or disorderly behaviour, or

    (b) displays any writing, sign or other visible representation which is threatening, abusive or insulting, within the hearing or sight of a person likely to be caused harassment, alarm or distress thereby.

**3.** It must be proved both that D intended to cause a person harassment, alarm or distress and that D's behaviour did in fact cause someone harassment, alarm or distress (*R v DPP* (2006)).

**4.** It is sufficient that there was someone near enough to hear the words: it is not necessary to prove that any person actually heard them (*Taylor v DPP* (2006)).

# 15.6 RACIALLY AGGRAVATED OFFENCES

**1.** If a defendant uses words identifying specific nationalities or races or ethnic background then this can make the offence an aggravated one within the definition of s28 of the Crime and Disorder Act 1998.

**2.** More general words such as 'foreigners' or 'immigrants' also come within the scope of s28, as in *Rogers (Philip)* (2006) where D used the words 'bloody foreigners' or *Attorney-General's Reference (No 4 of 2004)* (2005) where D used the words 'immigrant doctor'.

# INDEX